Toleration

KEY CONCEPTS

Barbara Adam, *Time*
Alan Aldridge, *Consumption*
Alan Aldridge, *The Market*
Jakob Arnoldi, *Risk*
Colin Barnes and Geof Mercer, *Disability*
Darin Barney, *The Network Society*
Mildred Blaxter, *Health, 2nd edition*
Harriet Bradley, *Gender, 2nd edition*
Harry Brighouse, *Justice*
Mónica Brito Vieira and David Runciman, *Representation*
Steve Bruce, *Fundamentalism, 2nd edition*
Joan Busfield, *Mental Illness*
Margaret Canovan, *The People*
Alejandro Colás, *Empire*
Mary Daly, *Welfare*
Anthony Elliott, *Concepts of the Self, 3rd edition*
Steve Fenton, *Ethnicity, 2nd edition*
Katrin Flikschuh, *Freedom*
Michael Freeman, *Human Rights, 2nd edition*
Russell Hardin, *Trust*
Geoffrey Ingham, *Capitalism*
Fred Inglis, *Culture*
Robert H. Jackson, *Sovereignty*
Jennifer Jackson Preece, *Minority Rights*
Gill Jones, *Youth*
Paul Kelly, *Liberalism*
Anne Mette Kjær, *Governance*
Ruth Lister, *Poverty*
Jon Mandle, *Global Justice*
Cillian McBride, *Recognition*
Anthony Payne and Nicola Phillips, *Development*
Judith Phillips, *Care*
Chris Phillipson, *Ageing*
Michael Saward, *Democracy*
John Scott, *Power*
Timothy J. Sinclair, *Global Governance*
Anthony D. Smith, *Nationalism 2nd edition*
Deborah Stevenson, *The City*
Leslie Paul Thiele, *Sustainability*
Steven Peter Vallas, *Work*
Stuart White, *Equality*

Toleration

Andrew Jason Cohen

polity

First published in 2014 by Polity Press

Polity Press
65 Bridge Street
Cambridge CB2 1UR, UK

Polity Press
350 Main Street
Malden, MA 02148, USA

ISBN-13: 978-0-7456-5556-7
ISBN-13: 978-0-7456-5557-4(pb)

A catalogue record for this book is available from the British Library.

Typeset in 10.5 on 12 pt Sabon
by Toppan Best-set Premedia Limited
Printed and bound in Great Britain by T.J. International Ltd, Padstow, Cornwall

The publisher has used its best endeavours to ensure that the URLs for external websites referred to in this book are correct and active at the time of going to press. However, the publisher has no responsibility for the websites and can make no guarantee that a site will remain live or that the content is or will remain appropriate.

For further information on Polity, visit our website: www.politybooks.com

For Timmy, with hopes that the world will become a better place in your lifetime and that you will continue to make it better.

Contents

Acknowledgments

Thanks to Emma Hutchinson of Polity for asking me to write this and for excellent advice during the process, including about how to improve the text. Thanks to Donna Cohen for encouraging me to accept Emma's offer and, more generally, for putting up with me. Thanks to all those with whom I have discussed these issues, including students, colleagues, friends, and family. Jim Taggart deserves special notice, as he's long been my most regular interlocutor. Dave Schmidtz and Chandran Kukathas also deserve special appreciation, Dave for an early career boost and Chandran for unwittingly setting me on the path of inquiry from which this book is a result. Three anonymous referees, Donna Cohen, Gerald Cohen, Cleo Grimaldi, Martin Lowenstein, and, especially, Sandy Dwyer and Heather Russel read drafts of at least parts of the book and gave useful – sometimes very useful – feedback, for which I am grateful.

Two other people are worth noting. First, Joel Feinberg, whose work on harm and the harm principle set the standard high for all future work on the topic. He would not endorse the view I offer here, but I hope he'd approve of the work nonetheless. Second, Jethro Lieberman, whose *Liberalism Undressed* (2012) came out while I was writing this book. I did not begin reading it until this text was complete, but I am very happy to have found another thinker who takes the harm principle to be the basic principle of liberalism (taking it to be much more useful than even Feinberg thought). Lieberman and I disagree about many points, but I am learning much from his book.

Introduction

In this book, I aim to provide a clear and lively introduction to the issues surrounding toleration. Debates about toleration have revolved around three issues. What is toleration? Should we tolerate and, if so, why? What should be tolerated? These questions are of central importance to moral and political thought. The last two are especially prominent in debates about how people should behave and how institutions should be arranged. They are the questions that motivate classical liberals like John Locke, Adam Smith, and John Stuart Mill. They thus also affect the work of all their intellectual descendants, ranging from contemporary welfare liberals like John Rawls to contemporary libertarian thinkers like Robert Nozick. Even the works of contemporary socialist thinkers like G. A. Cohen speak, though less directly, to these questions.

It is no exaggeration to say that the history of liberalism is the modern history of toleration. It was the first classical liberals – perhaps most notably John Locke – who argued for significant limits to the power of the state to interfere with its citizens. This was part of a shift in thinking about people living under a regime as *citizens* rather than as *subjects*. As subjects to a power, individuals could be interfered with at the will of the ruler. As citizens, they could not. As citizens, their lives were up to them and their choices – within some limits – had to be tolerated. I will not offer historical analysis or attempt to fully explain the most important thinkers in this tradition. Instead, I will concentrate on explicating the best answers to the central questions of toleration. While this will involve looking to historical thinkers along the way, the focus is on offering the best view.

A   Expectations and warnings

This book is not likely what you are expecting. To use a phrase, this isn't your Mom's introduction to toleration. Toleration is an often-misunderstood word – or, perhaps putting the same point differently, it is used in many ways without its users recognizing this. To begin, as I use the term, toleration is a behavior. If I want to refer to the related attitude (or virtue), I will talk of *tolerance*. But here's an interesting point: as we use the terms today, an extremely tolerant person can't tolerate very much. This is not to say that they seek to interfere in lots of other people's activities. It's to say that their lack of interference is not toleration. To tolerate, as we will see below, requires that one oppose that with which one does not interfere. This may be initially confusing.

This book may be different from what you would expect for a second, more important reason: as the author, I will not refrain from making judgments. As the reader, you will decide for yourself if my being judgmental is a problem. That is not my concern. I am concerned to help you understand and appreciate the idea and practice of toleration. And importantly, advocating toleration does not mean advocating some wishy-washy namby-pamby way of being that requires you to refrain from judging others. Why this is the case should be clear from what I said above: if you oppose nothing, you cannot tolerate anything. Those of us who oppose things – those of us who are judgmental, i.e., *willing to judge* – can tolerate things. Toleration, as we shall soon see, is *the intentional and principled refraining from interfering with another whom one opposes*. It is my hope that you believe or will come to believe that we should frequently tolerate others – not because we love, approve of, or even like them, but because we recognize that in a world where people oppose each other, toleration is a good thing. At least it's a better world than one in which we oppose others and don't tolerate.

So, a word of warning. We often want to express our openness to, or respect for, other cultures. That is, we want to be – and to be perceived as – tolerant. So, we might say things like "Well, it's not for me (or us) to judge," or "If they're OK with it, my view doesn't matter." However, a real commitment to toleration excludes any such relativist stance (see chapter 3C and, especially, chapter 7E). To be committed to toleration requires believing that toleration is a good thing and that *that* claim is not itself relative. We don't, I assume, want to say "Well since I think (or my community or culture thinks) toleration is a value, I won't judge anyone else – but, of course, that's relative to us, and if people in another culture don't accept it, they needn't tolerate us." Toleration *is* a value (see chapter 7); we *should* tolerate others and they *should* tolerate us (both with limits, as we will see in chapters 3 through 6). Moreover, there is an important difference between respecting a person (or culture) and respecting their beliefs.

Respecting someone does not require respecting his or her views. Showing respect for the person may even require that we challenge them (politely) when they hold views that are or seem unsupportable. While it's likely true that "they have *a right* to believe whatever they want," that does not mean that whatever they believe *is right*. Having a right to an opinion does not mean the opinion is right any more than having a right to property makes one rich – and we should not pretend otherwise. We should assume the people we meet are intelligent and worthy of our respect, but we should not be surprised to find that sometimes they hold *views* we cannot respect (we should still respect *the person*). There are good reasons why people – including very smart people – sometimes hold false views. (I hold several views that many people, some smarter than I, think are wrong. *You* may end up thinking I am wrong about a number of issues as you read what follows.) We can respect others, not respect their views, and tolerate their holding of false views. In fact, it would be decidedly *lacking respect* not to challenge at least some mistaken beliefs – it would be like saying, "Well, that person is worth-less anyway, so I don't care what falsehoods they believe." Rationally dialoguing with another shows respect – and is fully consistent with toleration. By the end of this book, I hope, you will be able to rationally defend your own view about what should be tolerated and why. (I also hope you will think my view basically right and so think we should tolerate very much more than we currently do – but that is a lot to expect.)

A final introductory note to those who think being judg-mental is necessarily bad: the very idea that we should not judge others seems to me very odd. Persons are rationally autonomous beings. As rational beings, we tend to evaluate things as we are exposed to them – at least the things that stand out to us (for whatever reason). That is what rational beings do. Rational beings do not, for example, merely sense the fallen tree in the road they are traveling on. They sense the tree and then evaluate the situation to determine what to do next. If they sense a man with a chainsaw standing next to the tree stump, they are naturally prone to evaluating that situation – perhaps judging that he must have either stupidly or maliciously caused the tree to fall onto the road. Persons, in fact, can't fail to judge – at least if they want to live well. Consider the man with the chainsaw. If he were wearing a white mask (à la *Jason Voorhees* from the *Friday the 13th* movies), it would be foolhardy to think, "Well, I shouldn't judge him – he may be very nice," and then to approach him in a friendly manner. This is not conducive to living well. One should judge that the masked man may be dangerous.

Though we sometimes fail to see it, we *want* people to judge others in all sorts of cases. We want criminals judged (and, perhaps, sentenced) just as we judge the man with the chainsaw. This is true in *many* areas of our lives. I don't want to read philosophy journals full of nonsense; I rely on the editors to judge the submissions they receive so as to publish only quality work. I most definitely want someone to judge the ability of people claiming to be medical professionals. And legal professionals. And chefs. And . . . the list goes on. We don't read things like *Consumer Reports*, *Zagat's*, or *Angie's List* without reason. We want someone to have done the work of judging. ("Who?" is an open question.) In many cases, we do the judging for ourselves. Often – I hope – we judge others positively or neutrally. Sometimes we judge them negatively. When we judge another negatively, we might seek to interfere with them. Other times, though we judge them negatively, we tolerate them and think everyone, especially the government, should do so as well.

B What lies ahead

Undeniably, there are different ways to divide the issues we shall be discussing. That said, the content and order of the following chapters seem to be apt. The first chapter introduces, motivates, and refines our topic. "Toleration" is a common word, but its use is often confused and confusing. It sometimes seems to be used as an excuse not to debate about important issues, for example, encouraging some to think "live and let live" no matter what and encouraging others to think there can be no facts about what it is OK to do. Both ways of thinking, however, fail to take into account what we all know – that there are limits to what we can and should let be. It is thus of the utmost importance that we clarify our topic and *why it is our topic.*

Chapter 2 explains a recent move in political philosophy to "strictly political" theorizing that is meant to avoid any metaphysical commitments (whether religious, moral, or other) and also to limit the domain within which the theory applies. This move has created a divide amongst political philosophers between those who accept it and those who do not. As I will explain, I think there is a middle ground that admits of some metaphysical commitments – though perhaps unlike those of other theorists – while endorsing the more limited domain of the political.

Chapter 3 introduces and explores the implications of John Stuart Mill's harm principle, which I take to be the most important normative principle of toleration (indicating the moral limits of toleration). That principle is widely known in political philosophy and normative jurisprudence, but is often overlooked as a source of justification for ending toleration. More to the point, it is often assumed that there are reasons

external to the harm principle that also justify ending toleration. I shall not endeavor to give definitive arguments against
such a view, but I shall endeavor to persuade you, Dear
Reader, to take seriously the possibility that it is only harm
that justifies interference. To do so, we must consider competing principles. Hence, chapter 4 provides discussion of other
influential principles of toleration and what would be tolerated if those principles were endorsed. The four discussed –
the offense principle, the benefit to others principle, the
principle of legal paternalism, and the principle of legal moralism – have all been politically influential. Indeed, all remain
politically influential to this day. The first three are defended
by intellectual greats in the liberal tradition of which this
book is part. I nonetheless would reject all of them, the fourth
as decisively as possible.

Rejecting those principles leaves us with the harm principle, which may seem to have an overly narrow focus. As I
think that is a mistake, chapter 5 extends discussion of the
harm principle to consider toleration's role in environmental
issues, animal liberation issues, cultural and international
issues, and the business world. It is here (and in the discussion
of the benefit to others principle in chapter 4) that this book
may be most novel. Many toleration scholars, in fact, are
likely to think the work misguided – especially when I push
to talk of tolerating poverty and the sorts of activities that
take place in the private marketplace. Perhaps perceived as
even odder will be the recommendation that while the harm
principle requires toleration of trades of sex and currently
illicit drugs, as well as of the outsourcing of labor and importation of goods, it also disallows much activity by US and
European corporations in other parts of the world – and,
indeed, may disallow corporations themselves. The further
recommendation that it is *we* who must interfere with – not
tolerate – such activities may also be met with incredulity at
first. Nonetheless, I urge you, Dear Reader, to take the arguments seriously and see where they lead. You may end up
disagreeing, but I hope you will find the arguments worth
considering. As I said, this is not like your mother's book on
toleration.

Speaking of mothers (and fathers), chapter 6 discusses
children – in the context of the so-called paradoxes of

toleration and liberalism. These paradoxes are intellectual puzzles. They are puzzles that encourage us to think of children. Children, indeed, are often the cause of much consternation in political philosophy. It is one thing to develop a fully worked out political theory about the relationship between an adult and the state, another thing entirely to work out the relationship between a child and the state. Importantly, for us, it is not clear that the harm principle can sufficiently indicate when toleration of activities affecting children should end. I shall argue, though, that it can. This is also an unusual claim.

The penultimate chapter of the book – chapter 7 – focuses on general defenses of toleration. This is, somewhat unfortunately, one of the longest chapters of the book. I consider this somewhat unfortunate as I am inclined to think defending toleration as a general value is not nearly as important as defending the right view of what should be tolerated. This will be clear by the time one reaches chapter 7 and I do not think it is that unusual a view now. Historically, though, it may well be an aberration. But only time will tell; my hope is that the focus for the study of toleration in the future is on the normative question – as it is in chapters 3 through 6. Despite my hope for the future, the arguments discussed in chapter 7 are important for us – some for historical reasons, some because they are cogent and convincing, and some because they are widely considered right (though those turn out not to be right!).

The book ends with a discussion in chapter 8 of why toleration is the first value of political society. Chapter 8 is nicely short – as I think concluding chapters should be. I'll say nothing more of it here.

Let us begin!

1

The Topic and Its Historical Relevance

A Reignland and some history

Imagine you live in the seventeenth century in a small but powerful country, Reignland. Reignland, like all other countries you know of, has a king. King Juris is fair and allows his subjects much freedom. Alas, though, Reignland was not always as pleasant. Less than 100 years earlier, Reignland was ruled by King Feris, an iron-fisted dictator. King Feris was fair, in a manner; he treated all his subjects equally (except his closest family, friends, and advisors – all of whom had much better lives than his other subjects). Treating his subjects equally did not mean treating them well. It wasn't exactly that he was cruel to them; it was more that he was extremely strict, in much the same way an overly strict parent is with a child. His subjects owned nothing, but held everything they possessed as a sort of lease from the King – and Feris could revoke that lease at will. For the privilege of holding such leases, subjects had to pay tributes – determined by the King's Court – to the King's Bursary. It was these revenues, of course, that made it possible for Feris to build castles, moats, roads, boats, etc. These did make life better for everyone. The revenues also made it possible for Feris (and his closest family, friends, and advisors) to enjoy the best wines, beers, chocolates, meats, spices, etc., that the world had to offer. Foreign merchants were frequently seen coming and going from Feris's castle. Most subjects, though, had no idea how good such luxurious foods were.

Most of Feris's subjects, indeed, had few ideas about the world more than a day's walk from where they were born. Feris did not allow his subjects to relocate without permission of the King's Court. When the people paid their tributes to the King's Bursary, it checked where they were living. Rarely were permissions given for relocation. Relocation, after all, would involve a great deal of labor from the King's Court. The Court would have to decide, after all, who could next live in the abandoned domicile, who would farm the abandoned land, whether the tribute needed to be adjusted while the newcomer settled, etc. Of course, the Court also had to decide where the requesting subject could be allowed to move, find them an existing abandoned domicile, or order a new one built, etc.

Life under King Feris was not terrible, but it was not good.

Things are different in your day. King Juris is the final arbiter and final power in the land, but his tribute rates are low and determined in advance in a way that is meant to be (and is – or at least is accepted by all as) both stable and equitable. As importantly, subjects own their own land and homes and can relocate simply by finding a buyer for their current home and buying another. There are even businesses that lend them money and places they can stay before finding a new home. All of this is remarkably different from life under Feris.

While life under Feris's reign was not terrible, it was limited. You had to do what people had always done; you could not experiment with different ways of living, different ways of making money to pay for your food and such, different ways to school your children, different ways of praying, different ways of dressing. In short, little was tolerated. By contrast, under Juris, you can experiment with different ways of doing things. Indeed, you can do anything you like, if you have the means, so long as you do not harm anyone else. Only when you harm someone else do the officials of King Juris's government get involved – that is the principle of Juris, and Juris is effective in having it enforced. In short, much is tolerated. Murder, rape, assault, theft, and the like are not. You and other residents are generally grateful for this.

Though Reignland under Feris's rule was not terrible, most of us would prefer to live under Juris's rule. Most of us prefer to be free to do what we wish even if we recognize that there are limits to what we should be free to do. Most of us prefer that our choices and actions be tolerated. Though we often have a hard time considering ourselves the subject to be tolerated – we tend to think we are good, should be liked, and that no question of tolerating *us* arises – this clearly can't be true for all of us. Many of us have been or are in situations wherein others do not want to tolerate us.

History is full of cases wherein some sought, or had, the power to interfere with those whom they believed were acting badly, even where the actions of those others had no bearing on anyone other than the actors themselves. Perhaps most famously, religious leaders have often sought the power to force individuals to accept their faiths, whether those individuals already had faiths of their own or not. Indeed, two of my own intellectual heroes (Baruch Spinoza and Pierre Bayle) faced religious persecution – lack of toleration. Others – including the government in one case – did not refrain from interfering with them but actively interfered with how they led their lives. They lived in countries that were, in important ways, like Reignland under King Feris.

For much of the early history of toleration, the primary concern was *religious* toleration. The question was simply "What religions should be tolerated?" If a country was Roman Catholic, for an important historical example, the question was whether to tolerate the practice of non-Roman Catholic religions (or non-Christian religions, or atheism). Non-Catholic nations faced the same question: should other religions be tolerated? In both cases (and others), if toleration was desired, the states also had to consider what toleration required, which is to say, what should be allowed and within what constraints it should be allowed. Some argued, for example, that toleration is consistent with forbidding public displays of particular religious practices as well as differential taxation, so long as no one was physically harmed or forced to give up their religion. Others argued for more extensive permissions. Significantly, toleration in such contexts is one-sided; the question is whether the powerful should tolerate the powerless (or less powerful).

The two heroes just alluded to lived in these circumstances. Consider the case of Pierre Bayle, an early defender of religious toleration. Bayle was born a Protestant in seventeenth-century France, a Catholic country. In itself, this was not that bad – though Protestants were the minority and suffered some disadvantages, they were not in terrible positions. But Bayle actually converted to Catholicism as a young man – for a short time. When he reverted back to Protestantism, he was a relapsed "heretic," and in a far worse position politically than if he had never adopted Catholicism. He thus left France (returning once before leaving for good). His writings drew scorn from both the French (Catholic) authorities and important Protestant theologians. The former imprisoned Bayle's brother, who then died in jail. There is little doubt his arrest was directly related to Bayle's "heretical" writings. The French were willing to tolerate Protestants, but not one who rejected (what they considered) the true religion after accepting it, no matter how briefly.

Consider now Baruch Spinoza. Spinoza was born a Jew in seventeenth-century Amsterdam, an extremely tolerant country by seventeenth-century standards (perhaps even by today's standards). The fact that Amsterdam tolerated religious minorities is important. The minorities were largely left to take care of their own internal issues – subject, of course, to certain limits. Spinoza was tolerated by his country. He was not tolerated, though, by the Jewish community into which he was born – he was excommunicated. The reasons for his excommunication (a rarity in Judaism: there is some debate if that is what the action amounted to) are unclear, but we know two things. One, he lost his inheritance because of it (the religious court had to realize that this would be a result since the act required that members of the group have no dealings with him). Two, Spinoza's later writings about metaphysics and God are decidedly out of line with mainstream Judaism (then and now). It may well be that he was already giving voice to the views he later articulated in writing.[1]

I do not want to give the impression that what happened to Bayle or Spinoza was insignificant, but the fact is, both were mere drops in the bucket of religious intolerance. There is no reason to go into detail about the history of the topic. I assume everyone is familiar with the Christian Crusades, the sixteenth-century religious wars in France, the Spanish Inquisition, and the witch hunts in both Europe and the Americas. In each case, one religious group sought to interfere with – even eradicate – the religious actions and beliefs of another. (Sometimes without evidence that there were such actions or beliefs!) We might think these issues have no bearing on us today, but this would be shortsighted, as will become clear.

Perhaps no one reading this will think that Christianity, Judaism, Islam, Hinduism, Buddhism, etc., should even elicit the question "Should it be tolerated?" It's clear enough, though, that some do ask the question, though perhaps in more narrow ways. Should a Muslim Mosque be allowed near Ground Zero in New York City? Should we tolerate abortion when the true religion (whichever one the speaker favors) claims it is murder? These questions appear frequently. Moreover, one might ask why there has never been a non-Christian president in the US. (Perhaps non-Christians are tolerated, but not *accepted* – a view I will briefly return to in the next section.) Of course, toleration is not just about religion. Should we tolerate rap music? Sugary pop music from manufactured boy bands or glamour girls? More seriously: cigarette smoking? gay marriage? cross-dressing? home-schooling? religious refusals of health care for children? eating – or sacrificing – animals? euthanasia? assisted suicide? The list goes on, and I have not even begun to consider international issues.

All the issues just mentioned have something in common: there have been suggestions that each should not be tolerated. Perhaps some should not. But *why* they should or should not is a big question. The bulk of this book will address it. But we also might wonder why we think it is such a big question. We might wonder, that is, why toleration *matters*. In one way, the answer should be obvious if we are talking about politics: non-toleration will mean the state using its considerable power against individuals, imposing its will on them. Indeed, at one point in time, this was the norm. It was only in the seventeenth and eighteenth centuries, after all, that toleration began to be seen as a value in its own right. This was a time when people were beginning to question their government's right to rule – and to dictate what individuals could do. This is the beginning of liberalism, classically understood (think John Locke and Adam Smith). These thinkers claimed that individuals were what mattered and had rights and could do as they chose, subject only to specific *justified* limitations. They could believe what they wanted about religion, for example. Bayle and Spinoza, mentioned above, defended that view. So did John Locke and others. It is now standard, but it wasn't then. Still, the origins of the belief are older.

One of the earliest Catholic theologians, St Augustine, put forward one of the most historically influential arguments for religious toleration some 1600 years ago. The basic idea of Augustine's argument is that because genuine religious faith cannot be forced, individuals must be tolerated so that they might attain salvation. A key premise of this argument is that genuine religious belief is only possible if it is freely (and, on some versions, rationally) adopted. Given the additional premises that genuine religious belief is necessary for salvation and that salvation is a good thing, the conclusion is that we must not force people to believe and so must tolerate. On an alternative formulation of the argument (spelled out by Jeremy Waldron (1988) who attributes it to John Locke), the means available to the state are necessarily coercive, so given that genuine religious belief cannot be coerced, it is irrational to seek to use the means of the state to encourage belief. Hence, toleration is required by reason. The problem with the Augustinian argument (in either version) is that there is clear empirical evidence that force can be used to put people in situations wherein they come to freely accept claims they previously rejected. For this reason, Augustine himself recanted his prior acceptance of toleration of heretics. He saw former heretics (the Donatists) accept orthodoxy when persecuted and believed that defeated the argument. Fortunately for us, later thinkers – early liberals like Spinoza, Bayle, and Locke – sought to offer further arguments in defense of toleration. We will consider some of these in chapter 7. (Augustine's argument is considered further in 7C.)

B   The concept

Thus far, I have been primarily working with a simplistic understanding of toleration as noninterference. This is the intuitive notion that most of us share when we only briefly consider the idea. Noninterference seems to be *the point* of toleration; that is, an act is only an act of toleration if non-interference is its *intent*. With further consideration, however, it is clear that "intentional noninterference" is not satisfactory as a definition of toleration. It's important that we get a bit clearer about our topic. Asking what should be tolerated without being clear about what it is to tolerate seems to put the cart before the horse. Clarity is clearly a virtue when discussing issues like this. If we are to say we should (or should not) tolerate a certain behavior, we need to know what we are prescribing. For our purposes, we will make do recognizing three conditions of genuine toleration. The first of these is intentional noninterference, as just discussed. But not all intentional noninterference is toleration.

Imagine your best friend is listening to your favorite music. You sit down and listen. It occurs to you that you might turn the music off, perhaps as a joke, perhaps because you think your friend should do something else. That would interfere with his playing the music. You decide not to. That is, you intentionally refrain from interfering and continue listening. We would not, I think, say that you are tolerating the music. Intuitively, you are not tolerating, but enjoying. Enjoying something makes it conceptually impossible to tolerate it. This suggests that some element of opposition must be present for noninterference to count as toleration. Most academic philosophers, in fact, think this is a necessary condition of toleration. Some believe that mere opposition is not enough and that it is *moral* opposition that is necessary – that is, they think we can only tolerate what we morally disapprove of. According to such thinkers, I might be able to tolerate students who refuse to work at school since I morally disapprove of that behavior, but I would not be able to tolerate students listening to bubble-gum pop music since my disapproval of that behavior is non-moral (the disapproval is aesthetic only). This is admittedly a question of ordinary usage: would we say that I tolerate listening to bad music or would we say something else? I am frankly not sure what else we would say. *I* would say I tolerate it. Given that intuition, I will assume the broader understanding of toleration in the rest of this book: what is needed is some form of opposition, not necessarily moral opposition. Even simple aesthetic distaste will suffice to make toleration conceptually possible.

There are a few who claim that opposition is not necessary for toleration. They claim a society that truly tolerates the cultural differences of its citizenry *cherishes* those differences. These thinkers, though, would admit that they are pushing for a "broader language of toleration" (Creppell 2002: xii) than we get with the "literal sense" of the term in contemporary thought (Galeotti 2002: 11).[2] What these authors seek, though, can easily be given voice in plainer language: multiculturalism. They seek to encourage societies to *accept* or embrace the differences that contribute to the fabric of social interactions. This seems to me an admirable goal (perhaps too admirable, but I'll say more about that in chapter 7H), but not toleration. Moreover, there is something odd about insisting that one must cherish what one tolerates. After all, I cherish my 3-year-old son and if you asked me if I tolerate him, I would think it very odd. I love him, I don't even consider tolerating him (though I may tolerate certain of his actions). I do not even refrain from interfering with him. On the contrary, I actively intervene to help him become a good person (which sometimes requires letting him choose badly). Similarly, multiculturalists presumably seek to help multiple cultures thrive – intervening if necessary to do so. If we want to say cherishing others is part of toleration, we might also need to say interfering with others is part of toleration. This takes us pretty far afield of ordinary usage. In the rest of this book, then, I will assume – what most agree to – that toleration is only possible where there is some opposition. As indicated, I will not assume the opposition must be moral in nature.

Thus far, I have said that toleration is intentional noninterference with something opposed. This should raise a simple question: if what is tolerated is opposed, *why* is it tolerated? Put differently, what is the reason to refrain from interfering with something that one opposes? Will any reason do? If we dislike or disapprove of the activity we tolerate, there must be a reason we tolerate it. Hence the third necessary element of toleration: there must be a *principled reason* for the non-interference. Not just any reason will do. Noninterference that is the result of laziness, fear, or a hope that something worse will befall the other when they are left alone, is no more toleration than noninterference that occurs without intention.

So what counts as a principled reason for our purposes? Perhaps the most common suggestions are the following three, related, possibilities: rights, individual autonomy, and respect. The idea for each of these is fairly simple. If we oppose someone's action, but (a) they have a right to do the action, (b) they must be allowed to act on their autonomy, or (c) they are worthy of our respect, then we cannot interfere *even though we oppose* the action. These can, of course, be easily conflated: we respect them because they are autonomous or because they have rights; they have rights because they are autonomous, etc. Importantly, though, we sometimes tolerate beings that we do not think are autonomous, deserve respect, or have rights. We tolerate nonhuman animals on occasion, for example. Perhaps the rabbit is eating the vegetables we planted outside and we decide not to interfere because, although we oppose the rabbit's actions (those are my vegetables after all!), we believe there is value in the natural order of things. We believe, that is, that noninterference with nature is itself a value. Given this, I shall say that the principled reason one does not interfere when one tolerates must be either respect for the other or the other's autonomy or rights or a principled belief that toleration (or one of its conditions) is *itself* a value. This is a broader view than some take.

The three primary elements of genuine toleration should now be clear: for P to tolerate X, P must intentionally refrain from interfering with X, P must dislike or disapprove of X, and P must have a principled reason for noninterference. As I argue elsewhere (see Cohen 2004a), there are additional elements, but for our purposes the three central elements suffice. Before endorsing these three elements, though, one should ask oneself if they are correct. Might we tolerate, for example, if we interfere only to constrain but not to completely disallow an activity? Might we tolerate by actively interfering *to aid* the tolerated? Might we tolerate because we cherish what we tolerate? Might I tolerate others because I don't want to be bothered with doing anything to prevent their actions? I believe these questions are all answered in the negative. Any policy that constrains, interferes – and so does not *tolerate* as we use that word today. Of course, we might seek to actively interfere to aid others we cherish, but this would not be toleration. If we tolerate, we intentionally refrain from interfering with something we dislike or disapprove of. If I refrain from interfering in such cases because I can't be bothered, I may be resigned, but I am not tolerating. King Juris might tolerate because he thinks of those who live in his regime as autonomous or rights-holding citizens, worthy of respect. King Feris, by contrast, thinks of those who live in his regime as *subjects* – that is, beings *subject* to his rule because not of the same importance as he, whether because not autonomous, not rights-holding, or simply unworthy. He may refrain from interfering, but such action on his part is unlikely to be toleration.

A final precursor to the rest of this book is in order. I have just spoken about kings tolerating their subjects or citizens of their realms. Readers of this book will not be living under kings (in the classic sense; constitutional monarchs are not kings in the same way as Feris or Juris). What will be important for *us* is the question when we, as individuals, ought to tolerate and, of course, when our governments ought to tolerate. The latter creates a small problem, since the first primary element of genuine toleration is *intentional* refraining from interfering and governments are not the sorts of things that *intentionally* do anything – they have no intentions at all, since they are not thinking beings. Similarly, the second primary element is that the tolerator must dislike or disapprove of the tolerated and governments do not have dislikes or disapprovals – again, because they are not thinking beings. So it might seem that governments cannot conceptually tolerate and we need to use different terminology when governments do not interfere in individuals' behavior. I suggest that when we think of state or government toleration, we are using colloquial language to say something somewhat more complicated. What we are saying is that the government has a policy against interference by state agents with the behavior in question. State agents that actually oppose the behavior in question might be tolerating (if they refrain from interfering on principle). State agents that do not oppose the behavior in question do not tolerate it, but they also do not interfere with it (in accord with their own inclinations as well as the state policy). A state, S, then, tolerates X, if it is the policy of S that all agents of S refrain from interfering with X, whether or not they dislike or disapprove of X. Presumably, the legislators in S have a principled reason for requiring that noninterference (and have incorporated that reason into law). Presumably also, there are some in the state who oppose the behavior in question (though it may be that no agents of the state do).

Given an understanding of what toleration is, conceptually, we can move forward to discuss what should be tolerated and why – as well as the general value of toleration. Before moving into that territory, though, we must discuss a recent division amongst political philosophers.

2
Two Approaches to the Normative Issues

This is primarily a work in philosophy, though it has obvious connections and relations to political science, jurisprudence, and other fields. Political philosophy today is what it is because of the work of John Rawls. For better or worse – and I think it is primarily for the better – Rawls has set the terms of the debates in political philosophy since 1971. This is not to say that all political philosophers agree with Rawls about everything. Most don't, though it is likely that a majority would endorse something like a Rawlsian view (in at least one of its incarnations). In any case, to do political philosophy seriously today, one must grapple with Rawls's work. Given this, an excursion into Rawlsian thinking will be helpful. This is complicated by the fact that Rawls's career can be thought of as having two distinct parts. It is common, today, to talk of "the 1971 Rawls" and "the 1993 Rawls." Rawls himself thought of his two projects as continuous – and I think this is accurate. I also think, though, that the second project has no necessary connection to the first. Importantly for us, the two projects may result in different approaches to what should be tolerated.

To prepare for what follows, consider the following scenario. In Reignland, there is a group, called Quinwanians, who believe they must grow and use quinoa (a nutritious grain-like crop) as a staple in their diet. Most Reignlandians, on the other hand, use wheat and corn and few even ever try quinoa. In Athforagia, a nearby kingdom, the majority of people engage in very little agriculture; they are an athletic people, happy to forage for their meals in untamed territory (they eat many small animals, some large animals when they have large gatherings, and many berries and other naturally occurring fruits and vegetables). There are, though, also some Quinwanians in Athforagia. Reignland and Athforagia have a long history of trade and peace together, but also a mutual distaste for each other. Most Athforagians consider Reignlandians a bit too sedentary and weak, while most Reignlandians consider the Athforagian ways a bit barbaric. We have here three groups: the majority of Reignlandians, the majority of Athforagians, and the Quinwanians.

Each of the three groups in our little scenario has a long history of considering social justice. Each believes that all people should be able to access adequate nutrition (perhaps they talk of it as a *right*). The Reignlandians believe everyone should be able to access the wheat and corn they need to survive; the Athforagians believe everyone should be able to forage as they please, and the Quinwanians believe everyone should be able to access the quinoa they need to survive. (Each thinks the other groups' preferred food choices at least odd.) They all agree, though, that adequate nutrition – whatever that is – should be available. The three groups agree about this, though for different reasons. The Quinwanians believe it because their religious texts specify it as a divine command, the Athforagians believe it because they take pride in their history and culture of athleticism, and the Reignlandians believe it simply because they think suffering is obviously bad and lack of nutrition leads to suffering.

Now ask yourself this: should what we tolerate be determined by (a) objective principles defended with arguments that are rationally independent of religious or ethical belief systems, or by (b) looking to existing belief systems and determining what their advocates can agree to? Putting the point in a very different way: should we accept a view about toleration that is derived from anything other than consensus? If you think (a) is right, you should think something other than consensus is the right way to go; if you think (b), you should think consensus is the way to go. Given the scenario above, if you think (a) is right, you should think there is some objective reason adequate nutrition should be available to all; if you think (b) is right, you will not be concerned to find such a reason, but will seek to demonstrate that all three groups accept "the principle of adequate nutrition" (that nutrition should be available to all) regardless of why they accept it. Whether you accept (a) or (b), you might be happy to use the principle of adequate nutrition in developing a political theory.

If you do not yet see the substantive difference – perhaps because you think there is an objective reason to endorse the principle of adequate nutrition regardless of what the three groups think – consider instead what you would think if all three groups had reason to believe that female circumcision was required of all female children, to be performed on them at the age of 8. Or if they all had reason to believe every third child a woman delivers should be sacrificed in a volcano. That the three groups would be able to reach a consensus on either of *these* views doesn't, I hope you will agree, indicate they are right (see chapter 3C for more on this question). Similarly, that the three groups can reach consensus on a principle of adequate nutrition does not indicate that such a principle is right. The motivation behind (a) is just that: that there is a truth of the matter regardless of what groups of people would or do agree to.

Importantly, in Rawls's early work, he seems to be an advocate of (a); in his later work, he is clearly an advocate of (b). Given his importance in political philosophy in the English-speaking world, it is not surprising that many have followed him in insisting that we seek consensus in endorsing political principles, including principles of toleration. As will be clear, I think this is a mistake. More clearly, I think there is a middle path that allows that there is something greater than consensus – but that also gains much of the benefit the later Rawls sought, at least where toleration is concerned.

It is important that the debate between those who follow the later Rawls in seeking consensus amongst existing belief systems and those who seek something more than consensus is not a debate about the normative limits of toleration. It is logically possible that, despite their differences, the two sorts of political philosophers can *completely* agree on what should be tolerated and what should not. As we will see, though, it may seem that those seeking consensus will tolerate more. Certainly, they will tolerate more than some of their opponents. Again, though, that is not the primary difference. The primary difference is simply that while one group seeks truth, the other seeks agreement. Some will clearly prefer to seek agreement – after all, agreement seems like something we can attain and truth may seem impossible to even identify (see chapter 7D and 7E). The Quinwanians, after all, believe their sacred texts are literally true so believe all must have adequate access to quinoa, but they have no success at all in persuading their compatriots in either Reignland or Athforagia of this. And neither Reignlandians nor Athforagians have had any better luck convincing the others of what they believe. Yet they can all accept the principle of adequate nutrition. In general, my guess is that political types would find agreement a more palatable pursuit, noting that it is hard to convince people of truth even if it could be found. They might also think that we have found a way to avoid having to convince people of truth.

Derek Bok has said that "[w]hatever one thinks about the intellectual merits of the positions taken by liberal philosophers, it is hard to regard them as plausible measures for a democratic government to adopt," and that their criticisms of various policies, while perhaps accurate, "are of little help in defining a set of practical steps to improve upon the status quo. On this score politicians have done better," especially as they have, "[o]ver the years . . . arrived at a rough-and-ready consensus" (2010: 87, 94). Bok is, needless to say, not a philosopher (and he seeks consensus at a different level of debate than do followers of the later Rawls). Regardless of what one thinks about the intellectual merits of Bok's claims – I think them too short-sighted myself, since it was philosophers who introduced liberalism, toleration, and democracy to the world – there is an interesting point here. If consensus is what helps improve the world, consensus may be what we should seek. Still, some of us prefer to seek the truth and to defend it even when we face opposition. Perhaps Bok and others are more realistic.

Historically, political philosophers did not concern themselves with either the politicians' or political scientists' tasks, but with something like finding the *best form of legislation* – we might understand it as seeking the truth of the matter regarding what legislation *should be accepted.*[1] The move made by the later Rawls – and many others since – can be understood as a move away from that sort of pure or ideal philosophizing to a form of philosophizing somewhat more interested in agreement – that is, (b) from above. Philosophers engaged in this task do not seek to get "votes" for their views by voting for what their philosophical colleagues prefer. Instead, they seek to find views that can be favored by all reasonable people, even if different people have different reasons for supporting the views in question. So, for example, the Reignlandians, Athforagians, and Quinwanians have different reasons for favoring the principle of adequate nutrition, but can be shown to be committed to that principle in light of their own belief systems. Philosophers that think (b) is the best approach, point out (like Bok), that the ideal philosophy that others have practiced does not seem very *helpful* in the real world – in fact, it seems distinctly detached from the real world. They think they can have a greater impact – undoubtedly a very big advantage – by finding a core set of principles, perhaps less than ideal, that all can agree to. That is, they seek consensus.

A Comprehensive doctrines

Recall again King Feris and King Juris. I did not indicate if either endorsed a specific religion. Imagine now that while King Juris is agnostic about religion and the existence of God, King Feris sets the laws of Reignland in accord with the requirements of his religion, Reigniosity. Reigniosity had been the dominant religion in the territory for centuries and every king therein endorsed it as the official state religion. Reigniosity has specific views about, and requirements for, how people should live their lives. They must, for example, pray to God every morning at sunrise and every evening at sunset. They must also do no work until an hour after prayer time and must neither raise nor eat any grains other than wheat and corn. Etc. In short, Reigniosity includes specific beliefs about the existence of God, God's powers, the relationship between each of us and God, and beliefs about how we must comport ourselves throughout our lives. Reignland under King Feris – as under his predecessors as far back as anyone can remember – is a religious kingdom.

King Feris, recall, is – in his way – fair. Indeed, he actually tolerates non-Reignion religions in Reignland. He treats religious believers all alike (except his family, friends, and advisors, of course, who benefit from far better treatment). Indeed, as Feris and his priests read the Reignion texts, this is required. This is not the case in all kingdoms of Feris's day. In many lands the state tolerates no religions other than that endorsed by its King.

King Feris endorses what we would now call a *comprehensive doctrine*. There are two defining features of such theories: (1) they have metaphysical commitments, whether explicitly recognized or not, and (2) this commitment affects what one's theory says not only about a narrowly circumscribed political realm, but about the wider social order. We are told that a doctrine is comprehensive "when it includes conceptions of what is of value in human life, and ideals of personal character, as well as ideals of friendship and of familial and associational relationships, and much else that is to inform our conduct, and in the limit to our life as a whole" (Rawls 1993: 13). A political theory based on Reigniosity has requirements, for example, about what grains one can eat – as hinted at above. A Catholic comprehensive doctrine, for a different (and real) example, would not only speak to the sort of government that is justified, but also to issues concerning abortion, church attendance, contraception, etc. Its verdicts on these issues would be rooted in its commitment to a particular theological view. Plato's comprehensive view would be very different from that, with a commitment to a particular view of the rational soul that required certain sorts of activities be practiced and certain other sorts of activities not be practiced. Hobbes and Locke each had still different comprehensive doctrines. Importantly for our purposes, classical liberals – those most committed to toleration in the centuries preceding ours – also are thought of as having comprehensive doctrines. Locke, Kant, and Mill are perhaps most important in this regard. Each had a commitment to a metaphysical view of the person that led them to their political conclusions – and more. Most classical political philosophers were committed to comprehensive doctrines.

As should be clear from what I've said about Feris's comprehensive doctrine (his religion, Reigniosity), that one endorses a comprehensive doctrine – whether it be religious as in Feris's case or moral as in Kant's case – does not require that one be unwilling to tolerate those who reject that doctrine. Of course, historically, there have been many comprehensive doctrines that did require that. But that is a factor of particular comprehensive doctrines, not essential to their being comprehensive doctrines. Classical liberals like Locke and Mill were advocates of toleration, though they also accepted – indeed accepted as grounding of their political views – comprehensive doctrines. They accepted what we can call "comprehensive doctrine liberalisms," each grounded in a different comprehensive doctrine.[2] The early Rawls did similarly. His work had certain grounding assumptions and it – supposedly – set requirements for a broad domain of human life because of those assumptions. We will return to this below.

B Rawls's strictly political philosophy

In his already classic *Theory of Justice* (1971), John Rawls was committed to a particular view of the individual person or self. Critics (in the 1980s especially) argued that his conception of the self was misguided and indefensible. The most common complaint (in this regard) was that he assumed that individuals could conceive of themselves as themselves *but without any of their actual commitments – to others or their goals.* That assumption, it was claimed, ignored our essential connection to others and did damage to that connection (see, in particular, Sandel 1982, but also MacIntyre 1984 and Taylor 1989, and, for different reasons, Young 1990 and Pateman 1988).

Although Rawls denied that he was ever committed to such a view of the self (see Rawls 1977: 165), his more extended response, developed over the next 20 years (culminating in his 1993 book *Political Liberalism*) seems to indicate he stepped back from his previous commitment to a comprehensive doctrine (at least he seemed to step back from claiming that such a commitment was necessary for liberalism). His later view is meant to be more accommodating to the reasonable diversity of metaphysical (including moral and religious) views (about the concept of the person among other things) present in modern society.[3]

In his "strictly political" liberalism (1993: xv), there is meant to be no commitment to any metaphysical conception of the person – it is *strictly* political, not based in anything pre- or nonpolitical. Instead, there is an attempt to show how a legitimate state – one that has the moral authority to make and enforce law – is one wherein anyone committed to any reasonable comprehensive doctrine (including any doctrine with a definite view about the concept of the person) would agree to the core principles guiding the state. Those core principles, then, stand free of any comprehensive doctrine and are the subject of an "overlapping consensus" of the existing "plurality of reasonable yet incompatible comprehensive doctrines" (1993: xvi).[4] In this way, Rawls's hope is to free political philosophy from any contentious beliefs – especially about the nature of the self. This maneuver, it is thought, makes the just state stable. The stability is expected to arise from the legitimacy derived from the core principles being agreeable to all (or all reasonable) persons. Advocates of communal religions as well as Kantian or utilitarian moral theories could all rally around these principles. We won't discuss those principles here – Rawls suggests they may be the same as those defended in his earlier work (see 1993: 291ff; but also see 1999: 581) – as we are not here discussing justice (or the whole of justice anyway).

Rawls thinks of his strictly political liberalism as *extending* toleration, saying it "applies the principle of toleration to philosophy itself" and that "[t]o apply the principles of toleration to philosophy itself is to leave to citizens themselves to settle the questions of religion, philosophy, and morals in accordance with views they freely affirm" (1993: 10, 154). This is an admirable project. After all, those with competing comprehensive doctrines can either seek to show each other that they are right and everyone else wrong, or they can seek to live with each other in peace. If it turns out that the competitors agree on some core set of political principles though they accept those principles for different reasons, then perhaps they can agree to keep their public activities within the range of those justified by those core principles. This would be nothing short of magnificent. The domain of the political would be curtailed, within that domain all would abide by the core principles, and outside that domain all would be free to live according to their own comprehensive doctrine (subject only to the proviso that they not violate the core principles).

It should be noted that if strictly political liberalism is meant to be a project about what should be tolerated – as Rawls sometimes suggests – it cannot be that the competitors just discussed simply agree to disagree so as to avoid conflict. Mere conflict-avoidance is surely not a principled reason that would undergird toleration. If I witness a crime and refrain from interfering only because I am afraid that involvement would leave me in a conflict I cannot win, my refraining from interfering is not toleration. Nor is it toleration if I know I can win, but simply prefer not to expend the energy necessary to interfere. Indeed, Rawls himself rejects a view wherein competitors engage in mere conflict-avoidance, what we call *modus vivendi* liberalism, wherein all live according to liberal principles, but wherein each would impose their own rules on others if only they thought they could get away with it. It is of the utmost importance to Rawls's later view that all within the state who are committed to reasonable comprehensive doctrines have principled reasons *from their own comprehensive doctrine* to endorse the core principles. This is meant to provide the liberal society with an element of stability it otherwise might lack.

The issue of stability clearly vexed Rawls. The important change in his views can be put this way: in the early work, he is concerned with determining what justice requires; in the later work, he is interested in what makes a political society, with its principles of justice, legitimate. In these terms, the later work seeks to show how the principles of justice defended in the early work could be part of a legitimate political society – a society wherein the government held genuine authority so that citizens could recognize themselves as morally obligated to obey the law. This would make the society stable.

Hence, we have one set of arguments (culminating in 1971) for an understanding of justice, and another set (culminating in 1993) for an understanding of how a society that is just according to that (or any) understanding of justice can be legitimate.

Those of us interested in toleration must grapple with the question of whether political philosophy can be "strictly political" in Rawls's sense. Toleration is treated differently in political liberalism than in a liberalism that is part of a comprehensive doctrine. In the rest of this chapter, we consider how toleration manifests in both and whether advocating toleration provides us with a reason to endorse a political or a comprehensive liberalism. In the process, we will also consider a variety of possible comprehensive doctrines, though we will not be able to discuss any in depth.

C   Comprehensive doctrine liberalism vs. strictly political liberalism

What we have seen in this chapter so far is that there are now two approaches amongst political philosophers regarding principles of justice – including, I suggest, principles of toleration. Which of those approaches we take affects what we say about toleration. So let us consider the two approaches.

When one approaches political thought with a comprehensive doctrine as a grounding, one seeks principles of justice that can be defended from that grounding. Ideally, though, such an argument is meant to be applicable to all persons, regardless of *their* concerns and commitments. Hence, political philosophers who take this approach seek to make their argument *rational* and accessible to all – i.e., one such that any rational person would assent to the principles of toleration or (more broadly) the principles of justice claimed to be true in the argument's conclusion. For this reason, the grounding assumptions in political philosophy are generally meant to be widely accepted. Still, given that we all have our own concerns and commitments, comprehensive doctrine liberalism recognizes that some people will not accept the defended principles of justice because those principles require – either as a grounding or as a consequence – the truth of some proposition that those people reject (or the rejection of some proposition they cling to), perhaps reasonably, given their other commitments. The fact that some people might reject such principles is recognized but not thought to bear on the truth of the principles. After all, the commitments that cause such people to reject the principles may be false so that well-informed, rational individuals should not maintain them.[5] Thinkers who take this approach are committed to finding true (or the most rationally defensible) principles, and in so doing accept some metaphysical commitments, generally as part of a comprehensive doctrine. (To be clear, one can be committed to some such claims without endorsing a comprehensive doctrine, but one cannot endorse any comprehensive doctrine without commitment to some metaphysical claims.) What those commitments are varies and may affect the variant of liberalism espoused. Those commitments, though, ground the principles of justice – including the principles that dictate what the state can interfere with and what the state must tolerate.

According to the strictly political view, no comprehensive doctrine can dictate how individuals must live in a polity. Advocates of this approach seek to avoid (when discussing politics) any metaphysical commitments and also to limit the domain within which their political theory is meant to apply. (To be clear, each advocate may have her own metaphysical commitments that give her reason to endorse the legitimate principles and that guide her actions in all domains, but she cannot insist those commitments are shared or should determine how others live.) Strictly political liberals insist we can do without metaphysical foundations as long as we have a freestanding conception of liberalism that can be endorsed by anyone committed to a reasonable comprehensive doctrine, even though they endorse it for different reasons. They also believe that the freestanding conception will thus justify legal interference in a narrow realm (because it is part of many reasonable comprehensive doctrines, it can only justify interference in the arenas that *all of those* doctrines would accept interference in).[6]

To focus our debate here, let's consider a particular form of comprehensive doctrine liberalism. The standard version considered by most – certainly most who endorse strictly political liberalism – is that wherein the individual self is considered to be autonomous, where it is not always recognized that different theorists define autonomy differently. On this standard view, autonomy must be protected and promoted in a just society. Let's narrow this sort of doctrine further, to a form of liberalism that is part of, or accepts, a comprehensive doctrine that includes a belief that all polities should be arranged such that all citizens are encouraged to lead autonomous lives, whereby they determine for themselves – with no input from others – what moral, political, spiritual, and religious beliefs to hold. Put differently, on this caricature, liberals believe that each and every individual sets (or should be able to set) her own values by herself without any regard for, or relation to, others, and also believe that friendships and familial relationships can only have value if they are freely chosen by all the participants. Call this the *atomism* thesis. The idea is that each of us is (or should see ourselves as) completely separate from all others when choosing our values. Atomist autonomy, it should be clear, is an extreme version of autonomy. It is unlikely that any historically important liberal held such a view, but that is not important here. (Locke is often criticized for holding such a view, but he clearly did not. On his view, we are born "blank slates" that our parents and others "write on," by providing us with experience.[7])

It would hardly be surprising if there were intelligent people in a given society who found themselves unable to endorse the caricatured atomistic view just described. If it were part of the political view meant to animate their state, they might find themselves at odds with the state. This may be even more the case if the atomist view is thought to be the best way to defend the state's liberalism. "If defense of or commitment to liberalism requires *that*," they may think, "so much the worse for liberalism." They may think of themselves as fundamentally part of a community they did not and could not choose. A religious community, for example. Perhaps they believe that God's plan requires that all have freedom, but that all exercise that freedom within the comforting confines of the religious community. Such freedom may be limited by those confines – perhaps one must pay a tithe to support others or perhaps one cannot be a practicing homosexual – but otherwise be quite extensive. Despite the extensive commitment to freedom – including, let us assume, freedom of speech, bodily integrity, political participation, and association – those committed to this religion would not be able to endorse the state's version of liberalism. They may even find themselves arguing against the state's commitment to atomism as encouraging vicious behaviors likely to come from those who do not recognize themselves as fundamentally members of a community.

Strictly political liberals may seem to have an advantage here, in that they accept a principle of political legitimacy such that "exercise of political power is fully proper only when it is exercised in accordance with a constitution the essentials of which all citizens as free and equal may reasonably be expected to endorse" (Rawls 1993: 137).[8] This means that those in the religious community just discussed (assuming it is a reasonable religion) would be able to endorse their state's version of liberalism. (Interestingly, if the principle of political legitimacy is not accepted *as true*,[9] we seem to have a *modus vivendi* view only – which Rawls would reject – and if it is accepted *as true*, this second approach is not as far from the first as it would otherwise seem.) On this view, we do not seek true principles of justice to determine what the state can and cannot do; we seek principles that no one could reasonably reject. The state can only interfere with activities if such principles allow it. Put more simply: the state can interfere in activity only if principles – whether true or false – allowing such interference would be acceptable to all reasonable citizens, including members of reasonable religious groups.

Strictly political liberalism, again, seems to have an advantage over comprehensive doctrine liberalism, as endorsement of a particular comprehensive doctrine (whatever it is) closes certain questions, with the doctrine providing what are taken to be true answers to those questions. The comprehensive doctrine liberal will assume that where others disagree with those answers, they are mistaken. The atomist autonomist liberal, for example, claims that the best way of life is the atomist autonomist way of life. All other ways of life are somehow less valuable. By virtue of being deemed less valuable, perhaps, they are not tolerated. That is too simple, but it gets to the point: autonomy is promoted and, in promoting autonomy, ways of life that do not value autonomy (or do not value it as much as the motivating comprehensive doctrine requires) are not, so the thought goes, tolerated (really, they are just valued less; whether they are tolerated or not remains an open question).

Given that the comprehensive doctrine liberal claims to have true answers to questions about how to live, she seems to endorse state action in a broader arena then the strictly political liberal. She seems willing to *not* tolerate in a greater array of situations. For the autonomist liberal, for example, the state should have policies designed to make it likely that all individuals will become autonomous. If this means requiring lengthy mandatory schooling, so be it. If this means disallowing subservience in the home, so be it. If this means disallowing voluntary arrangements of any sort where one individual is treated as less than fully autonomous, so be it. This is extensive interference in the private lives of individuals. Strictly political liberals, by contrast, can allow that individuals can take on subservient roles in private, so long as they retain their *political* autonomy. They can affirm liberalism in the public sphere while simultaneously working for "other values in nonpublic life" where they "may regard their final ends and attachments very differently ... They may regard it as simply unthinkable to view themselves apart from certain religious, philosophical, and moral convictions, or from certain enduring attachments and loyalties," presumably even to individuals they treat as their superiors in private (Rawls 1993: 31). In short, autonomist liberalism seems unwilling to tolerate private relationships wherein one party is subservient to another, but political liberalism seems willing to tolerate such relationships – at least as long as all individuals are recognized as autonomous and as "self-authenticating sources of valid claims" (Rawls 1993: 32) in the public arena.

Some may wonder (*should* wonder) if that last clause has the strictly political liberal taking back much of what he was supposed to be gaining. After all, if there is a relationship wherein one party is – presumably consensually – subservient to the other (whether because of religious beliefs about the status of women, or because of some sexual predilection, or whatever) that subservience is likely to carry over into the public arena. While it is possible for Submissive Sunny to be submissive in her personal relationship with Dominant Don and not submit to Don in the public arena (and for Don not to seek such), it is also very easy for those roles to have weight in all areas of Don and Sunny's life, such that for example, Sunny seeks Don's instructions at the voting booth as well as the bedroom. She becomes used to taking his instructions – and him to giving them – and doesn't consider bracketing that for public activity. If this is something the political liberal will seek to correct, its effect may be to encourage Sunny's autonomy in all areas of her life – and the view seems no longer so *strictly* political.

The problem is not limited to isolated cases of those in domination-submission relationships. Nor is it even limited to such individuals and those in religious groups that leave men and women with different statuses. The problem, indeed, is widespread in any modern Western society that has attempted universal education. If the state is committed to guaranteeing that all its citizens are politically autonomous, it will provide an education that is conducive to such autonomy. If children receive an education that includes "such things as knowledge of their constitutional and civic rights so that, for example, they know that liberty of conscience exists in their society and apostasy is not a legal crime" and that "prepare[s] them to be fully cooperating members of society and enable[s] them to be self-supporting," as Rawls indicates (1993: 199), they will receive the tools and impetus to question the belief system of their family and group. While the purpose, for Rawls, is "to insure that their continued membership [in their religious or cultural group] when they come of age is not based simply on ignorance of their basic rights or fear of punishment" (1993: 199), the fact is that there will likely be an accompanying byproduct or spill-over effect whereby they have the wherewithal needed to be fully autonomous. Indeed, Rawls grants that this is possible, but considers it unavoidable and acceptable (1993: 200).[10]

Given what we have just seen about the strictly political liberal approach, it would seem that the limits of toleration according to that approach are not likely much broader than those of autonomist comprehensive doctrine liberalism.

I will not set out to prove this, since I do not endorse an autonomist liberalism. I do endorse a comprehensive doctrine liberalism, but it is a "thinner" version – that is, one with fewer commitments. As we will see, it does not require endorsing the promotion of autonomy for all. In the rest of this book, (part of) my own comprehensive doctrine liberalism will become clear.

What is important about comprehensive doctrine liberalisms for our purposes is that they involve a commitment to finding the most defensible (hopefully, true) normative principles of toleration, independent of their acceptance by any group of people. Fully rational people, after all, sometimes have powerful reasons for holding to views they cannot prove or defend and rejecting more defensible views. Rawls himself shows us this clearly with his talk of the "burdens of judgment" (1993: 55–7). These epistemological concerns are very real and should not be ignored, of course. But the comprehensive doctrine liberal believes that they need to be addressed *after* the best normative principles of toleration have been determined. Only with those principles on board is this sort of liberal likely to suggest that the time arrives for the strictly political concern of "selling" those principles in the polity so that they are adopted not only by the state, but also by groups and individuals within the state. Putting this point differently – and in a way that may be important for those studying political philosophy more broadly – the comprehensive doctrine liberal is concerned first to do ideal theory to determine the true principles and only then to enter the domain of the non-ideal to figure out how to institute those principles in a society where people are not already complying with them. So we turn now to the project of seeking the most defensible – hopefully true – principles of toleration.

The last sentence is intended to make clear that I take myself to be a comprehensive doctrine liberal, dealing with principles of toleration that are defensible independent of any consensus. The sort of liberalism I defend, though, takes true principles of toleration to only give guidance for a narrowly circumscribed set of activities, not a broad domain of human life. We might think of this as a "thin-theory comprehensive doctrine," since it is (intentionally) not "thick" enough to speak comprehensively. Put differently, the view is something of a middle ground between other comprehensive doctrine liberalisms and a strictly political liberalism in that it does endorse specific metaphysical commitments – different from those of other theorists – though it also endorses the more limited domain of the political. It requires extensive toleration – certainly more than the autonomist liberal and perhaps more than the political liberal. The real difference with the latter, though, is not in the extent of toleration it requires (though it may be greater). The real difference there is in its acceptance of a particular view of the individual and its willingness to endorse certain principles as true regardless of consensus.

3
The Harm Principle

A The question

Arguably, the most important question of political morality is "What should be tolerated?" In a world where people disagree, disapprove of things others do, and simply dislike others, some will be motivated to interfere with the way people live their lives. It is sometimes easy to tolerate other people and their behavior; it is sometimes quite difficult. The moral quality of what we tolerate is not always what makes it easy or hard. We might even have difficulty tolerating *morally praiseworthy* behavior, when, for example, our family members give money to charity that we think they should use for themselves (or worse, for us!). Sometimes, tolerating morally bad behavior is fairly easy. Lying might be bad, but we frequently tolerate it simply because interfering would be too onerous. (If we only refrain from interfering for that reason, we are not tolerating. Toleration requires a principled reason; still, the difficulty could provide a supplemental motivation not to interfere.) Of course, some acts are so heinous that everyone agrees we must not tolerate them. Murder and rape are like this. Yet other questions of toleration are the subjects of intense debate. Some think we must tolerate prostitution, pornography, homosexuality, and same-sex marriage. Some think we must not. Some think we must tolerate abortion, cloning (or research aimed at cloning), stem cell research, assisted suicide, and euthanasia. Some think we must not.

One helpful way to frame these debates (and many more) is to be armed with principles that indicate what should and should not be tolerated by indicating an underlying factor whose presence suggests toleration is inappropriate. If X is present, toleration is required. Alternatively, if X is present, toleration is forbidden. More likely, if X is present, not tolerating is permitted. But what might X be such that it unifies all cases? What would make a case such that it was permissible to *not* tolerate?

As should be clear from the examples in the first paragraph of this section, the moral value of toleration does not mean everything should be tolerated. This is reason to think we need normative principles of toleration: principles that indicate when toleration is required and when its normative limits have been transgressed. With such principles in our philosophical arsenal, we can raise the level of debate from "Should this particular act here and now be tolerated?" to "First, what are the correct principles indicating when toleration is required and, second, do those principles indicate that we should tolerate this act here and now?" This would allow us to be systematic in deciding what to tolerate. In this chapter and the next, I discuss five historically influential principles that have been defended by legal and political theorists. I begin, in this chapter, with the most important and most defensible. Everyone accepts some version of this principle: the harm principle. In the next chapter, we discuss four others that, in my view, should be rejected, but that are nonetheless influential.

As a reminder, the approach of this and the next two chapters is that of a comprehensive doctrine liberal: seeking to defend normative principles of toleration independently of any consensus (though with the hope that such principles will gain support since they are rationally defended). While one or more of the principles discussed in this chapter and the next may be such that all would accept them, my concern is with their rational defensibility, not consensus. The strictly political liberalism defended by the later Rawls and his followers, by contrast, believes that legitimate normative principle(s) must be in accord with all the reasonable comprehensive doctrines accepted in society. While there may be reason to think that being in accord with those doctrines suggests that the principles are true (see J. Cohen 2009), this can only be a secondary issue for the strictly political liberal. Putting this point differently, the advocate of political liberalism must accept the outcome of political deliberation of all reasonable comprehensive doctrines. If the outcome of that process is endorsement of principle X, he must accept principle X. This also means, though, that if the outcome of the process is endorsement of principle X in all situations except where conditions of type C occur, he accepts that. The advocate of political liberalism, then, does not really endorse particular normative principles of toleration; he accepts as morally required whatever tolerating acts are endorsed by the process of political deliberation of all reasonable comprehensive doctrines and he rejects those that the process rejects.[1] The strictly political liberal can only see these principles as useful rules of thumb.

B   Introducing the harm principle

Philosophers, political theorists, and jurisprudence scholars have offered many normative principles of toleration. Normative jurisprudence is, in fact, largely a search for such principles. Joel Feinberg enumerates nine (1990: xix–xx). The first of these is the topic of this chapter: John Stuart Mill's famous *harm principle*.

Mill tells us that "The sole end for which mankind are warranted, individually or collectively, in interfering with the liberty of action of any of their number is self-protection . . . the only purpose for which power can be rightfully exercised over any member of a civilized community, against his will, is to prevent harm to others" (1978[1859]: 9). The basic idea is that harm is always a prima facie reason to permit interference, whether to prevent its otherwise imminent occurrence, to penalize those who cause it, or to rectify its damage. No one wants to be harmed. Allowing interference – non-toleration – to prevent it is a good idea.

The basic idea of the harm principle, it should be clear, is fairly noncontroversial. The harm principle itself, though, is controversial. This is because if we take Mill seriously in the passages where he provides the principle, he tells us that harm is the *sole* end justifying interference, the *only* purpose that offers such justification. If there is no harm, on that reading, there is no cause for interference. Let us call the harm principle that excludes other justifications for interference (where "only" and "sole" are emphasized), the *strict version* of the principle. There are other, less strict, versions – including Feinberg's – that allow for the endorsement of other principles, some of which we discuss in the next chapter.[2]

According to the strict version of the harm principle, it seems that *helping* some is not cause for interference with others. Providing basic welfare goods to poor people may be praiseworthy, but if we take the "only" seriously in the original version of the harm principle, it seems we will not have justification for interfering – with taxation, for example – with any individuals in order to be able to provide those goods to others. Indeed, if we take the harm principle in its strict form seriously, there would be a very limited class of things we would not tolerate. For example, we would have no justification for interfering with, and so must tolerate, all of the following: prostitution, pornography, homosexuality, same-sex marriage, abortion, cloning (or research aimed at cloning), stem cell research, assisted suicide, and euthanasia. At least, we would have to tolerate each of these in all cases except those where it can be demonstrated that harm would be caused – and then we would have justification for interfering in those cases only. I should be clear that I think this is right – all these things should prima facie be tolerated if opposed (I actually do not oppose any of them). State policies regarding these things should be policies of toleration.

Of course, some will undoubtedly argue that abortion necessarily causes harm to the unborn fetus. If that case can be made, it would be permissible to not tolerate abortion. Furthermore, it is likely that in any of the other examples in the list just provided, a harm *could* be caused. Engaging in sexual relations with a prostitute could cause real and presumably harmful damage to one's spouse and marriage, for example. We'll discuss these sorts of issues further, but must handle another task first.

C Harm (and objectivity)

The harm principle – in the strict form – will be endorsed in this chapter, but will first need to be clarified. Most importantly, we will need to explore the use of the term "harm." A tree branch falling on you after a storm is likely to hurt you, but we are unlikely to think that the harm principle is to be invoked in such a case. There is no one with whom we could possibly interfere to prevent or rectify the harm. We cannot arrest the tree (or the storm!) for harming you – and all would recognize trying to do so as foolhardy. If Tom accidentally bumps into you in the hallway, causing you to bang your arm on the wall, we would also be somewhat unlikely to think he should be arrested or even scolded (perhaps he should apologize). Again, the harm principle does not seem relevant. It is important, then, that not all occasions where someone is *hurt* trigger the *harm* principle. This means that "harm" must be understood here to have a narrower meaning then it ordinarily has. Not all hurts are harms as that term is used in the harm principle. I will follow Joel Feinberg's analysis of the sort of "harm" that is relevant to the harm principle as a *wrongful setback to interests* (see, e.g., Feinberg 1984: 36).

Harms, for the purposes of the harm principle, are wrongful setbacks to interest. What does this mean? There are, obviously, two elements to the idea: *wrongfulness* and *interest-setback*. Readers will likely be concerned with the first of these and perhaps also with the second. Rightfully so. These are difficult and controversial concepts.

To determine if there is a harm as that term is used in the harm principle, we have to determine if there has been a wrong. Many people in our society apparently think that whether a particular act is wrong cannot be determined objectively. Many, indeed, seem to think it is a purely subjective matter: if I think the act is wrong, it is wrong for me; if you think it's not, it's not for you. Others think it is a cultural matter: our society thinks the act is wrong so it is wrong for us; yours does not, so it is not for you. I think this is misguided – and for much the same reason I think we should reject political liberalism in favor of the correct comprehensive doctrine liberalism. We should be seeking truth where that means "objective truth." "Subjective truth," so far as I am concerned, is an oxymoron, a contradiction in terms. If a proposition is true, it is true for all. It makes no sense to say "well, its true for me, but not for you." How am I supposed to understand such a claim? I can certainly understand the claim that "I believe its true and you do not." There we simply have differing opinions. But the truth of a claim does not depend on my opinion or your opinion or even *our* opinion.[3]

Consider the claim "God exists and is omni-beneficent." Some people believe this. Others do not. Does the fact that they have different opinions matter? Before answering that question, notice that we don't seem to hear debate about the presupposition behind the question: it is a *fact* that there are different opinions. We take this to be *objectively true*, not subjective. That is, we do not say "well, it's true for some people that some (but only some) people believe there is a God and false for other people that some (but only some) people believe there is a God." Such a statement would be met with incredulity. In fact, if the statement were accepted – it never is, so far as I can tell – we would face the same question at the next level: is it a fact – objectively true – that "it's true for some people that some (but only some) people believe there is a God and false for other people that some (but only some) people believe there is a God"? Or is that claim subjective so that it's true for some people that *it's true for some people that some (but only some) people believe there is a God and false for other people that some (but only some) people believe there is a God* and false for other people that *it's true for some people that* some *(but only some) people believe there is a God and false for other people that some (but only some) people believe there is a God*? The mind boggles at such a question. Of course, the issue gets even crazier if we ask if that claim – the above sentence with two italicized clauses – is itself objectively true or not. Apparently, there are some claims that we all agree are objectively true. The obvious claim here that we all take to be objectively true is that people have different opinions about the existence of God.

Now return to the question that began the last paragraph: does the fact of differing opinions – and I now assume we all agree *that* is a fact – matter to the objectivity (or lack thereof) of the claim that God exists? Let me cheat here and simply switch the burden of proof: *why would it matter* that there is disagreement? Of course, I do not mean that question very broadly; it matters that there is disagreement about God's existence for very longstanding political reasons: some that believe do not want to tolerate atheists, perhaps some atheists do not want to tolerate believers, and clearly believers in different descriptions of God (which go along with different religions) do not want to tolerate believers in other descriptions. What I mean here is a very narrow question: what difference could it make *to the existence of an all-good, all-powerful, all-knowing God* that some believe he (or *it*) exists and some do not? I think put that way, the answer is obvious: *none whatsoever*. It is either the case that God exists or it is the case that he does not. One of those is the objective truth – which means also that the disjunction ("God either exists or he does not") is objectively true. If he exists, atheists are wrong; if he does not, then theists are wrong. There is an objective fact of the matter even if we do not *know* what that objective truth is. *Our lack of knowledge of the truth has no effect whatsoever on the truth.* (Why would it?)[4]

Now come back to the subject of this chapter: harm and the harm principle. We said that harms as understood in the harm principle are wrongful setbacks to interests and we realized there will be disagreement about whether or not particular acts are wrongful. We can now say that such disagreement – which is, of course, very real – has no effect on the wrongfulness of an action. Either an act is wrongful, or it is not. If the act is wrongful and also a setback to interests (which we will discuss in a moment), it is a harm and the harm principle allows us to stop tolerating and interfere. If the act is not wrongful, it is not a harm – whether or not it is a setback to interests – and the harm principle requires that we not interfere, and instead, perhaps tolerate.

So harms are wrongful setbacks to interests. What is a wrong? Granted, now, that an act is objectively wrongful or not, how do we know if it is a wrong? That, admittedly, is a very difficult question. Answering it would take us well beyond the limits of this book. Answering it requires doing in-depth moral theorizing, including work in metaethics and epistemology. I highly recommend taking courses or reading good books on those topics, but we can't go into them here. Fortunately, we do not need to. As it turns out, the great ethical theories of the world tend to agree about most acts. Whether it be the utilitarianism of Bentham, Mill, or Sidgewick, the deontology of Kant, the eudaimonism of Aristotle, or any of the world's religions (Judaism, Christianity, Islam, Hinduism, Buddhism, etc.), there is widespread agreement that, for example, murder, rape, and theft are wrongful. And almost all agree that helping others is not wrongful. Of course, there is debate about the status of some acts – abortion comes readily to mind – but we should not let the (admittedly fierce) debate about a few issues blind us to the widespread agreement. Murder is wrong and should not be tolerated. Helping others is not wrong and so must be tolerated. Listening to pop music, as banal as it might be, is also not wrong and must be tolerated. Etc.

OK, enough now about wrongs. But what is a setback to interests? This is also not as clean as we might like. Importantly, as with wrongs, there are some obvious cases. Murder is obviously wrong and it obviously sets back the victim's interest in continued living (and the interests of friends and family in having the victim alive). Theft is obviously wrong and it obviously sets back the victim's interest in controlling her resources for her own purposes (and her interests in those purposes). If you punch me, my interest in not feeling pain is obviously set back. Admittedly, not everyone has an interest in not feeling pain. Some enjoy pain. Those who actively seek to join a "fight club" likely do not have an interest in not feeling pain (at least, the pain caused by being punched). Masochists, of course, not only don't have the standard interest in not feeling pain (they may have an interest in not feeling specific pains), but actually have an interest in feeling (certain specific) pains. Nonetheless, we can assume that in the typical case, individual persons have interests in not feeling pain, in continuing their lives, in continuing to act as they decide to, etc.

We can't mask the fact that there will be difficult cases where we cannot easily determine if an interest is set back. Say you are rowing a boat and come across Flo floating in the water. Flo tells you she has been there for hours, since her own boat sank. She has been alternatively swimming and floating, hoping either that land was closer than she thought or that someone would come by in a boat. She is very happy to see you and moves to climb into your boat. If you do not allow her into your boat, are you setting back her interests? Obviously, you are setting back her interest in getting in your boat. But if she later drowns, did you set back her interest in continued living? It's tempting to say, "Of course!" but it's not so simple since in *not* letting her get on your boat, you didn't *do anything* that caused her to stop living. Her loss of life was caused by her sunk boat (and whatever caused that), but your action – or inaction – is at most a contributing factor. You might, in fact, act wrongly in not letting her get on your boat *even if you don't thereby set back her interests.* Perhaps you should let her on your boat, but her interests were set back before you even arrived on the scene. If this isn't clear, ask yourself if you set back her interest in continued living if you took your boat in a totally different direction so that you didn't see her at all. You were on a boat and could have looked for her, found her, and then saved her. But you went a different way. In so doing, did you set back her interests? Presumably not. But then why would your happening to see her set back her interests? (What if you saw her from a distance, sincerely thought "I don't want to bother Flo, she's clearly having a good long swim," and turned in a different direction?)

The problem laid out in the last paragraph is often called the *baseline* problem. When considering the case of floating Flo, we can't know if you set back her interests unless we know what the baseline of her interests is. In this case, we have to know if the condition from which we measure whether Flo's interests are forwarded or set back is the condition she is in when you found her (in the water without any flotation aid) or the condition that she is more typically in (presumably, not in the water). If the former is the baseline, you did not set back her interests. If the latter, you did. You didn't make her worse than she was in the water; you did contribute to her not being on dry land.

What should be clear at this point is that determining whether or not there is a harm (in the sense used in the harm principle) can be difficult. Often it is easy. If you come up to me and punch me in the face for no reason, you wrongfully set back my interest in not feeling pain. You harm me. If you take my wallet from my pocket without my permission, you wrongfully set back my interest in controlling my money. You harm me. These are paradigmatic cases of harms. If you give me a present of a first edition of John Stuart Mill's *On Liberty*, you do not harm me. You forward my interests, benefiting me. This is paradigmatically not a harm.

Paradigm cases are actually instantiated quite often. Murders, rapes, burglaries are almost always harms. Nonetheless, there are times when the case is unclear and we cannot be sure if there is a wrong or if there is a setback of interests. Recently, for example, an old man in my neighborhood killed his wife and then himself. In the typical case, this would have been a harm to his wife. As it stands, though, it was very clearly a mercy killing (and suicide because he could not stand to live without the love of his life). The man did not set back his wife's interests; in fact, he forwarded her interest in not living with the disease she suffered from. Arguably, he also did not wrong her. Admittedly, sometimes we cannot be sure if a particular act is a harm. If we can't be sure if it is a harm or not, we cannot be sure if the harm principle justifies interference or not. What do we do in such cases? We can't spend too much time on this question, but we should note two things.

First, we can (and often do) use paradigm cases to discuss, by comparison and contrast (arguing from analogy), unclear cases. We may be able to come to a rational conclusion by such moral reasoning. Second, where the interference that would be justified is burdensome, we need more certainty that there is a harm; where the interference is less burdensome, we need less certainty. If the interference is the death penalty, for example, we should be very sure there was a harm – we should be very certain that the person we are considering executing committed the act, that the act was wrongful, and that it set back the interests of the alleged victim. (There must be a *wrongful setback of interests*, not merely a wrong and a setback of interests.) We should be concerned to get some degree of certitude if the interference is a $100 fine, but surely it will be less troublesome if we are wrong in such a case. In my own view, once these two considerations are recognized, the default position is that there is no harm. That is, we assume there is no harm unless it has been shown, subject to some burden of evidence – which varies depending on the severity of the interference permitted – that there is.

The intuition behind Mill's principle should now seem straightforward: it is bad to be hurt and it is thus wrong to intentionally hurt another person unless there is a morally weighty reason to do so. I should not punch you when I see you on the street, but if tackling you to the ground is the only way to prevent you from being hit by a car, doing so will be permissible. The former is an unjustified – wrongful – hurt. It is thus a harm and should be prevented. The latter may be a hurt (when you hit the ground, it pains you), but it is justified rather than wrongful and so need not be prevented.

It should also be clear that the interference justified by the harm principle is likely to set back the interests of the individual interfered with. Given that, if we are culpably mistaken about there being a harm that justifies such interference, we may wrongfully set back the interests of the person we interfere with (say we execute someone mistakenly found guilty of murder – someone who is actually completely innocent of all crimes). Put simply, interferences that are only mistakenly thought to be justified may well be harms themselves. This is why there is a burden of proof that must be met. We want to prevent harms in the first place, so do not want the harm principle to be an excuse for doing harm. The harm principle justifies interference with someone who has done a harm – it basically says that the interference is justified rather than wrongful and thus not harmful. If we misapply the harm principle we may find ourselves committing a harm and thus in a position such that *we* should be interfered with.

D More on the harm principle (considering harm to self, etc.)

With the narrower understanding of harm, we can further elucidate the harm principle. Notice, first, that the harm principle is about harm to *others*. Interference designed to prevent an agent from acting on an intention that would affect (even hurt) only herself is not permissible according to the strict version of the harm principle. Indeed, there is a conceptual oddity about the possibility of harming oneself.

Harms, remember, involve wrongs. If I harm you, I necessarily wrong you. I can't harm you without wronging you. Similarly, then, I cannot harm myself without wronging myself. But how can I wrong myself? Just as a boxer is not wronged or harmed by his opponent (assuming the opponent fought fairly), it seems that I am not wronged or harmed by my own actions. In both cases, the reason for this is simply that when one consents to or welcomes an act done to oneself, the act can't be wrongful. Boxer Allen punches boxer Bobby. Bobby is not some uninvolved party, but a voluntary participant in the fight. He consented to the fight, which he expected would include him being punched. So he can't claim to be harmed. I work out at the gym and pull a muscle. I did so voluntarily – that is, I consented to the workout. I can't claim to have wronged myself. I was hurt, of course. I hurt myself. But my consent to the act means I did not wrong myself.

The idea that what one consents to cannot be a harm to oneself is embodied in the jurisprudential principle *volenti non fit injuria* – what one welcomes (or consents to) cannot be an injury or wrong (though it can hurt). When I say to you, a fellow member of my fight club, "Yes, punch me," I can't justifiably complain when you do so. Similarly, if I punch myself – perhaps to get my blood flowing – I can't justifiably complain "Bad me, I punched me." In both cases, I may be hurt, but as I consented, I was not wronged and thus not harmed.

If one cannot wrong oneself because one consents to one's own actions, someone else cannot wrong one if one consents to that other's actions. (Hence, the boxer.) If we adopt the harm principle as the sole normative principle of toleration, when two or more people act upon one another with full consent, their action must be tolerated. Importantly, though, we are assuming here – as is assumed in the harm principle – that the two (or more) individuals are what we typically call "adults." They are, that is, mature rational beings. This may not be clear from what was said thus far, but Mill is quite clear about this and we should – and I do – accept his view on the matter. In the paragraph following his rendering of the harm principle, he tells us: "It is, perhaps, hardly necessary to say that this doctrine is meant to apply only to human beings in the maturity of their faculties. We are not speaking of children, or of young persons below the age that the law may fix as that of manhood or womanhood. Those who are still in a state to require being taken care of by others, must be protected against their own actions as well as against external injury" (1978[1859]: 9). This is hardly an unusual limit. All societies distinguish between those who can be (held) responsible and those who cannot.

Once the distinction between non-rational or non-mature agent or child and rational adult is recognized, it should be clear that the harm principle applies only to rational, mature adults. We cannot justifiably interfere with an adult's choice to eat only hot dogs – no matter how foolish such behavior is. We can try to explain to them why the behavior is foolish, but if they are rational adults they are entitled to make bad choices (which they may think of as good or bad). Of course, we do not say the same of children. Parents would rightfully interfere with their child's decision to eat only hot dogs. And it's not just parents. Should you see a 5 year-old child chasing a ball into a busy street, you would be justified in interfering. Picking the child up and putting him down on the sidewalk and telling him not to run into the street is more than acceptable. It is desired. By contrast, with the adult, the most you could do is check to see that she understood the danger (more on this in chapter 4C).

From this brief discussion, it should be clear that just as someone too young to rationally consider the consequences of his actions can be interfered with for his own good even when no actual harm is involved, ignorance, deception, and mental defect can leave an adult (chronologically determined) in a situation such that interfering with him for his own good even when no actual harm is involved is justified. Ignorance, deception, and mental defect can render a person unable to consent even to his own actions; such a person should be treated as (perhaps temporarily) incapacitated and so without a rational or autonomous will. Interference is permitted not because there is a harm (there may not be), but because we are not talking about a rational person. We rightly interfere with animals, human children, and human adults who are mentally incapacitated when they are acting in a way that is likely to cause themselves hurt. We do not, though, interfere with rational adults who cause only themselves hurt. And, of course, that we can interfere to prevent a child or mentally incapacitated adult from hurting themselves does not mean we can interfere with them in just any old way. More on this in chapter 6B.

E Rational persuasion, permitted but not required interference, types of interference, and justice

It's important to note that when we talk about the interference that is warranted when one causes harm, we are not talking about rational persuasion. Rational persuasion may be useful in such cases, but it is not interference in the sense we are discussing here. Indeed, one can try to rationally persuade someone to act in a particular way or not to act in a particular way even where no harm is involved. If no harm is involved, according to the harm principle, we must not interfere. If we oppose what the other is doing, we have to tolerate their actions. Toleration, though, does not exclude rational dialogue (see Cohen 2004a: 74, 80, 86). This should, in fact, be obvious. No one thinks it wrong to try to dissuade a loved one from acting in ways that will leave him less well-off. Parents try to convince their children, siblings try to convince each other, and friends try to convince friends not to take actions that will leave them with interests set back. Sometimes we do this and point out interests the other did not even realize they had. We might say to Sara: "You should not go to law school, you are a great graphic artist and always seem happy when you are doing that sort of thing – go to art school, or look for a job in the field." She might respond: "Hey! I never thought of that, but you are right!" Our rational dialogue was permissible, even praiseworthy, and certainly not a failure to tolerate (nor was it toleration). Of course, if Sara responds "I see your point, but I want to go to law school," we can't sabotage her application process – that would be an unwarranted failure to tolerate. One consideration here is that sabotage can set back Sara's interests in a way that rational dialogue does not. Rational dialogue may set back Sara's interest in not considering alternatives, but it does not set back her interest in going to law school – she can freely continue on that path after the conversation. Successful sabotage, by contrast, makes that impossible.

Another important factor about the harm principle of which we must remain cognizant is that it does not answer all questions, even about interference with harm. In particular, it is important to realize that what the principle says is that it is *permissible* to interfere when there is harm – that this is when toleration rightly *can* end. It does not say interference is *required* in all cases of harm. Indeed, while minor harms may make interference permissible, we often think interference in such cases would nonetheless be a mistake. Imagine, for example, thinking that we should seek out the person who stole a single page out of my notebook. Yes, they harmed me – perhaps quite significantly if what I thought was a masterpiece of a poem or drawing was on that page (they stole it for a reason, after all!). My interest in presenting that masterpiece to my wife was completely set back – and wrongfully so since no one had any justification for taking my work. In such cases it is likely too costly to interfere. So we refrain from interfering though the harm principle allows interference. Notice that this is not toleration: we refrain because of the cost, not because of a principled reason. This will matter more in large-scale events like those we discuss in chapter 5B.

A final important point here is that though the harm principle tells us when interference is warranted, it is silent about *what sort of interference* is permitted. Plausibly, extreme physical force is permitted to stop a murderer, but not to stop the thief of that single page from my notebook. Similarly, it's plausibly true that harsher punishments are warranted for greater harms. But none of this follows from the harm principle directly. Some may think a complete theory of toleration would include indications of what sort of interferences are permitted in the various sorts of cases where interfering is warranted. If that is the case, this book does not offer a complete theory of toleration. I do not think that is the right way to consider the issue though, since interferences are, by definition, not acts of toleration, and the book is not intended to offer a theory of ways to fail to tolerate.

Chapter 5 will make clear that I have an expansive understanding of toleration. What I mean by that is simply that I believe a complete theory of toleration can do much more for our understanding of what justice requires than is typically thought. After all, it indicates when the state and others will justifiably interfere with individuals, groups, and organizations. If the state interferes in order to guarantee equal welfare, for example, it is not tolerating. Such a failure of toleration may be warranted, of course. If it is, then one's theory of toleration should indicate that state interference is warranted in such cases. Similarly, if a state interferes with the lives of murderers, it fails (clearly appropriately) to tolerate murder. If we figure out principles that indicate when toleration is not required – when some limit has been transgressed – we thus figure out much of what justice requires. Justice requires that we never interfere where toleration is mandated.

Despite my expansive understanding of toleration, even I would not say that a theory of toleration is a complete theory of justice – for the simple reason that while such a theory will tell us when interference is permitted, it *will not tell us what the right sort of interference* is. (It does, though, set some limits since wrongful interferences that set back interests will not be permitted as responses to harms.) A complete theory of justice must tell us not only when we can interfere, but also what sort of interference is then permitted. We rightfully interfere with attempted murder, but do we put the criminal in jail, kill him, or fine him? Toleration does not seem to speak to that, as none of the options is a tolerating act. (The harm principle does tell us not to harm the murderer – we can set back his interests, but must do so in a just way.)

Knowing what counts as justice in punishment will be important for a complete theory of justice.

F "Indirect harms"

Perhaps as a way of foreshadowing some of the argument in the next chapter, it might be worth briefly considering a final distinction relevant to harms. Mill labels the distinction with the terms "direct" and "indirect" harm, but those labels are problematic. The core of the distinction, according to Mill, is that "definite damage, or a definite risk of damage" places an act in the province of morality or law but "merely contingent" injuries do not (1978[1859]: 80). What he has in mind when he speaks of merely contingent or indirect injuries is clear from the surrounding text.[5] The concern is with the sorts of ways people set back the interests of others as a result of acts that are themselves in no way harmful to those others. For example, Billy might set back the interests of his bank when he gambles with money he had planned to use to pay his mortgage, and Jenny might set back the interests of her sister when she misses the latter's wedding because she was too drunk to leave the house, but neither Billy's gambling nor Jenny's drinking harms anyone. Billy's gambling might leave him unable to pay his mortgage, but it is that inability that leaves him wrongfully setting back the bank's interest, not the gambling (after all, had Billy gambled with other saved money, there would be no problem). Similarly, Jenny's being drunk does not wrongfully set back her sister's interests, though her failure to attend the wedding may well do so.

Some will think that Billy's gambling is a problem independently of the fact that it causes Billy to set back the bank's interests. They might think it is morally reprehensible or offensive. Similarly, some might think Jenny's sister is harmed because she loves Jenny and hates to see her waste her life – not merely because Jenny missed the wedding. These ideas will be explored in more depth in the next chapter, but here it is important that neither claim can be used to justify interference based on the harm principle. Those who think gambling reprehensible might have their interests set back when people like Billy gamble and Jenny's sister might have her interests set back when Jenny drinks too much, but in neither case has the person whose interests been set back been wronged. Assuming they did not have an agreement that she would stop drinking, Jenny does not wrong her sister because *she does nothing at all to her sister* (if they did have an agreement that Jenny would stop drinking, Jenny would have violated that agreement). Billy does nothing to those who hate gambling. He has no relationship with them at all. That they are hurt may be true, but they are not wronged – and hence not harmed – *by Billy*.

There are, unfortunately, often people who claim to be harmed by merely knowing that others engage in certain sexual acts (homosexual acts or premarital sex, for example). Although such "harms" may really hurt people with peculiar psychological states, those engaging in the sex acts in question *do nothing to them*. This is true even if they know that such people exist and will have interests set back merely by knowing such acts occur. If we claimed otherwise, we would also have to claim that those flying the space shuttle harm me should I think flying it reprehensible. The same would be true, indeed, for *any* acts that someone found so troubling that knowing they occur set her interests back. This would allow each of us to hold everyone else captive to our interests in a bizarre and extensive way. What we should say of such acts is, at most, that they hurt particular people who are sensitive in specific ways – but hurts are not necessarily harms. Since *no wrong is done to them* – even if they are right that there is a wrong done – they are not harmed. This is why Mill's language is problematic: indirect harms are not harms at all.

Consider Harriett, who is pained by the knowledge that there is homosexual activity, which she firmly believes is immoral. In discussing the harm principle, we do not have to determine if she is right about homosexual acts being immoral if it is clear that they are *not wrongs done to her*. Wrongs that are not wrongs done to specific people may warrant an end to toleration according to the principle of legal moralism (see chapter 4D), but not according to the harm principle – which is relevant only when one person wrongfully sets back the interests of another.

Mill's distinction is useful, but its usefulness is only in pointing out that for an act to be subject to interference according to the harm principle, it must be an act that is a wrong done by one *to* another. There may, though, be wrongs that are not wrongs to another – what we can call "free-floating wrongs." As we will see in the next chapter (especially 4D), some think such wrongs are enough to justify interference.

4
Other Principles

According to the strict version of the harm principle, harm *and only* harm justifies interference. Yet, while all believe that harm at least often justifies interference, many also believe that interference can be justified in some cases where no harm is present. They offer other principles that merit consideration. Some readers are likely to endorse one or more of these along with a (less strict) version of the harm principle that is modified so as to allow the additional principle(s). In this chapter, I discuss four such principles that have been offered to indicate when interference is permitted even when there is no harm in the technical sense: the offense principle, the benefit to others principle, legal paternalism, and legal moralism. While I think we should reject all of these, recent thinkers in the liberal tradition have admirably defended variants of the first three.

Since we assume that everyone would endorse the claim that harm to others is a good prima facie reason for interference, anyone endorsing an offense principle would be of the view that harm and offense, but perhaps nothing else, are always good prima facie reasons to interfere. Similarly, someone endorsing a benefit to others principle would be of the view that harm and benefiting others, but perhaps nothing else, are always good prima facie reasons to interfere. And so on for legal paternalism and legal moralism. Of course, someone could endorse more than two of these; indeed, someone might endorse all five (the four of this chapter plus the harm principle). So, for example, someone endorsing the offense and legal moralism principles would say that harm, offense, and (some) harmless immoralities, but nothing else, are always good prima facie reasons for interference. In any case, the reader is encouraged to take each of these principles seriously and consider which should be endorsed. As indicated in chapter 3, my view is that the strict version of the harm principle should be endorsed and that the remaining four should be rejected. My view, though, is not the final statement on the matter. Various thinkers defend various subsets of these principles and debate clearly remains. Readers are encouraged to judge the arguments independently. Differences of opinion here are possible and I have no intention of interfering with people who endorse any of these principles. Indeed, even if definitive arguments against the following principles were found (or created), I would tolerate people who mistakenly endorse them.

A   The offense principle (and psychological harm)

Joel Feinberg (1988) believes that offense can sometimes justify interference. He explicitly means to discuss things that offend without harming. What is it to *be offended, take offense, cause offense*? Do we think that all cases of offense warrant interference? Some people are easily offended. They might see a picture of a nude person and take offense. Others seem never to be offended. Call them the worst name you can think of and they barely respond. There are, though, some things that we all find offensive. To use Feinberg's example (1988: 11), imagine sitting on a bus. At the next stop, a couple board. Ten minutes later, they are nude. They do not immediately have sex, though. First they each defecate on plates. They then proceed to eat the feces along with strawberries and champagne – and have mad, passionate sex while spreading their picnic "delicacies" on each other. Most of us, I think, would find this offensive – for multiple reasons. Importantly, even if none of us was hurt in any way from this

Caligulan exhibit, most would think it should be illegal. If that is correct, then perhaps the harm principle must be supplemented with a principle that would allow interference.

So how do we distinguish cases of offense that warrant interference from those that do not? Put differently – and in a way meant to parallel our previous discussion of the harm principle – how should we understand "offense" in the offense principle, which claims that offense is a prima facie good reason for interference (that is, offense warrants non-toleration)?

As indicated by the fact that some people are more easily offended than others, there is clearly a subjective component to offense. You are offended by breastfeeding in public; I am not. I am offended by slang curse words; you are not. Which of these – if either – would warrant interference? Recall that harms are wrongful setbacks to interests. Recall also that wrongfulness is an objective factor, even if sometimes hard to determine. The same can be said about the sorts of offenses that warrant interference: they are wrongs. That is, unless there is wrongful offense, toleration is required. After all, we want to say of the couple on the bus that they do something wrong to the other passengers, but we don't likely want to say that the breastfeeding mother wrongs anyone. So, the view here is that wrongfully offending another is good prima facie reason for interference.[1]

There are many ways to be offended.

I lived for four years near poultry processing facilities (where live chickens and turkeys are taken and processed into the chicken and turkey you buy in supermarkets or restaurants). On certain days, the stench was rather unbearable. It was, we might say, *offensive*. We'd be hard-pressed, though, to say it *hurt*. It wasn't as if my nose burned when I breathed. For three years, I lived near an experimental farm. Others who lived nearby found the smells emanating from the farm offensive in the same way. These included typical farm smells: horse and cow manure, etc.

Some people take umbrage at the act of burning or otherwise desecrating patriotic images. Flag-burning in the US, for example, always evokes outcries. Some would ban – not tolerate – the act. Similarly, many find the artwork of Andres Serrano – who apparently put feces and other bodily fluids on various artifacts, including a crucifix – offensive in a way that makes it worthy of banning. The sacrilege is thought to cross a line.

Talk of "crossing a line" is helpful if only metaphorical. The idea is that there are some things that are so intensely, vividly, loudly offensive as to belong in a category of things that ought to be banned from spaces where they could not be avoided. Offenses in this category are extreme. They are also likely – as with Feinberg's coprophagic picnic on a bus – to be offensive to *everyone* (other than the participants).

The coprophagic picnic is intense. It is vivid. It is loud (metaphorically if not literally). It is unavoidable to those riding on the bus. Pornographic movies on television might be intense and vivid, but they can be avoided by changing the channel. The same is true, to a large extent, of public fornication. What we might say of those sorts of offenses is that they require active participation of the viewer to generate offense. Only if the viewer chooses to look at them can the viewer be offended. By virtue of the viewer's choice to view the items, though, we might also say that the viewer is not wronged (even if the items are nonetheless immoral – an issue I discuss in section D below). By contrast, if I am a passenger on that bus, I can't avoid the offense. I can't refrain from viewing the offense. It overcomes me. The actors are doing something to me – causing me offense. If I could walk away but choose to look, I seem to be complicit in the act – as if I am partly doing it to myself. On the bus, I cannot walk away. I am offended and I am wronged. Hence, according to the offense principle, toleration can end.

Should coprophagic picnics on buses be banned or tolerated? I imagine most would say they should be banned. But perhaps the question that makes that answer likely is oversimplified. Let's ask a slightly different question: should we tolerate or ban a group of people all of whom consent to take a bus ride together knowing that some will engage in a coprophagic picnic and knowing that the owner/operater of the bus line has agreed (presumably for a fee) to allow this to occur? The only people on the bus will be individuals who know what to expect of the ride and thus can be said to voluntarily participate in their being offended. It seems clear, that is, that *Volenti* removes any wrongfulness (or, rather, any wrongfulness to others on the bus). This is not, then, the sort of event the offense principle is meant to justify interfering with – for there is no wrong to anyone. If this is right, though, it seems that the wrongfulness aspect, not the offense aspect, does all the work in the offense principle. We're hard-pressed, I think, to find an event more offensive than what takes place on this bus. But it's not wrongful so it should not be interfered with – even if some who rode the bus were offended (perhaps they wanted to test themselves; perhaps they had an odd desire to witness things they find offensive).

In chapter 3, recall, we said that wrongs were not enough to warrant interference. Yet, here it seems that the wrongfulness to individuals in certain offenses does all of the work toward justifying interference. How can this be? To answer this question, let's look at two cases involving religion. Say Adam decides to defecate on a religious ornament in front of a group of people who take such treatment of that ornament to be sacrilegious. Perhaps he plans to defecate on a crucifix in front of a church. This seems offensive in a way that merits interference. Similarly, when Nazis marched in Skokie, Illinois in the 1970s, their actions seemed so offensive, especially to the Holocaust survivors who lived there, as to merit interference. I would suggest that in both these cases, there is a clear wrong: the attempt to belittle, embarrass, anger, or otherwise hurt a particular group of people who (let us assume) did nothing to deserve it. Adam seeks to hurt the Christian group and the Nazis in Skokie sought to hurt the Jews living there.

Notice that what is important in my description is that the actors *intended to hurt others*. They knew that the others would be offended and took action anyway. They were not merely negligent – they took action *in order to* hurt others who were, for all practical purposes, innocent. If that is not wrongful, I do not know what is. But notice something else – perhaps what you thought I was first drawing attention to. The intent was *to hurt*. Sometimes – perhaps often – when someone seeks to offend another, they are seeking to hurt the other. Indeed, it seems fairly easy to imagine that Nazis marching in Skokie would not only be offensive to the Holocaust survivors living there, but would also likely cause those survivors significant psychological suffering – psychological *harm*. If that is the case, interference is permissible according to the harm principle and the offense principle is irrelevant. Adam seeks to wrongfully set back the interests of the churchgoers and the Nazis sought to wrongfully set back the interests of the Jews in the Skokie community. As they seek to do harm, the harm principle clearly allows interference.

While physical pains and harms may be easier to assess, there is no principled reason to think there are no psychological harms. Nor is there reason to doubt that the harm principle allows for interferences to prevent (or punish a perpetrator of, or to rectify) these, though care will be needed to prevent slipping from psychological harm to mere offense.

What about the defecation on the crucifix in front of the church? Much the same can be said here. Those witnessing the act may well be psychologically harmed. In both cases, importantly, there are at least two sorts of psychological harms that may occur: there is the individual mental anguish that the witnesses suffer and, in all likelihood, another pain they suffer as members of a group. Let me clarify.

All of the Holocaust survivors living in Skokie are likely to suffer severe anguish when faced with reminders of the torment they faced in Nazi concentration camps, no matter what anyone else feels. Indeed, even if no one else knows Joe is a survivor and he knows this (so he can't think the Nazis are attacking him), he is likely to feel such anguish. Given that he *is* known to be a survivor, there is a second sort of pain involved: the fear of being attacked because of his group identity. That there was a community of survivors in Skokie, after all, is the reason the Nazis wanted to march there. The fear that was wrongfully induced by the Nazis may well be a harm. Indeed, both the fear that each feels individually though as members of the community and the anguish they feel independently of the community would be setbacks to their interests. They would quite reasonably say "I have an interest in having a peaceful state of mind, not being fearful, not having anguish." This interest is wrongfully set back. And the same is true of the crucifix case: some members of the church are likely to feel anguish at the thought that anyone would treat a crucifix this way and are also likely to feel the fear that comes when there is an attack on their church.

If what has been said thus far is right, it seems that in the cases of offense where interference is justified, it is justified by the harm principle. Indeed, we should wonder now whether anyone would have thought to prevent the Nazis from marching in Skokie if they thought no one living there would feel mental anguish or fear. And we should ask ourselves if we would seek to ban the act of defecating on a crucifix if no one witnessing it would feel mental anguish or fear or have their interests set back in any other way. If the answer is "no" – as I think – we have strong reason to believe the offense principle does no work at all. Toleration must hold unless there is harm.

Let's return, briefly to the coprophagic picnic on the bus. We said that if everyone involved consented, *Volenti* eliminates the wrongfulness to them and the offense does not justify interference. What if we return to the case where no one on the bus consented except the couple engaging in the act? My own view is that even here offense is not the real problem. People wear t-shirts on buses that are or could be construed as offensive, and we rightly tolerate this. That the picnic is *more* offensive does not seem particularly worrisome. There are, though, two very real concerns. First, some of us on the bus are likely to be so nauseated by witnessing this event that we become physically sick. The couple then causes us to be hurt – they set back our interest in remaining healthy and comfortable. This is true, I think, even if the suffered discomfort is only psychological, so that no passengers become physically sick but some suffer psychologically. If the couple wrongs those who are sickened – and it seems they do, since they have to realize their action would cause significant discomfort in other passengers and not significantly benefit anyone – they are harming those they sicken. For that reason, the harm principle is enough to justify interference, and the offense principle, again, does no work. Moreover (and second), it is likely that the couple will leave their excrement (and bodily fluids) behind when they get off the bus and this can spread disease. This would be a public health issue: the spread of disease that would hurt others, setting back their interest in health. Again, this seems like it would be wrongful (on the assumption that one should not generally act in ways that would predictably cause another hurt) and so harmful. So again, the harm principle justifies interference and the offense principle is superfluous.[2]

Some will disagree, thinking: "Look, in some of these cases it doesn't matter if there is an actual harm or not – some things are so offensive that they should not be tolerated on that ground alone. Defecating on the crucifix, for example. It doesn't even matter if no one sees it! It's offensive and should be banned." But can this be right? If there are no witnesses, there is no one to be offended (and no one to be wronged). Why is interference needed? It may be, but if it is, it is not justified by the offense principle, but by a principle of legal moralism (cf. Simester and von Hirsch 2002: 283), which I will discuss later (section D below). The idea there is that the act is simply immoral, even if no one is affected, and that immorality is warrant for interference. But if no one is affected, no one is offended and the offense principle is about offenses *to others*. Offense must be experienced to matter.

Mind you, there are many other examples we could consider. Cartoons of Mohammed in Denmark offended many Muslims. Assuming the cartoonist (or publisher) acted wrongfully, does this warrant intervention? Consider also *Jerry Springer: The Opera*, which many Christians found offensive. Does this warrant disallowing the performance? What if it was clearly being staged in order to annoy those Christians? Should it be stopped? What of Terry Jones's very public and very obnoxious burning of the Quran? I am unable to decipher the "Pastor's" intentions, but if he was committing his foul act merely to annoy Muslims, should he have been stopped? In each of these cases, my own view is simple and consistent with what I have said thus far: absent some demonstration of a harm, toleration must hold. Indeed, in each of these cases, I find it difficult to see what sort of harm could be claimed. In each case, the supposed victim could turn their attention to other things so that they would not be hurt or offended. As Feinberg would say, they could have reasonably avoided the offense (1988: 26).

Some worry that in the sorts of cases being discussed, failure to prevent the acts would result in riots such that people and property would be hurt (by the original actors, rioters, or intervening police). Hence, they claim, the harm principle allows us to interfere here just as it allows us to prohibit drinking and driving – to prevent a statistically likely harm. This is not, of course, any defense of the offense principle; it is, rather, an attempt to use the harm principle to argue for prevention of specific offensive acts. I think we must admit that if it could be proved that harms would result if (and because) a cartoon was published or a play enacted, it would count as good reason to prohibit the activity. We must also realize, though, that this is dangerous territory since anytime someone wanted another's act stopped, they would only have to truthfully say a harm would occur – even at their hands! – if the other's act were tolerated. Such blackmail must not be allowed. Martin Luther King should have been allowed to march; those threatening to cause harm if he was should have been stopped since it would be *them* causing harm, not him. Similarly, if a group of Muslims threaten harm should Terry Jones burn a copy of the Quran, it would be *they* whom should be interfered with, and if a group of Christians threaten to cause harm to prevent *Jerry Springer: The Opera* from being performed, it is *they* who should be interfered with. Put simply, the harm principle does not allow interference with just anyone; it allows interference with the one doing or likely to do the harm.

Before moving on, I should note that the view expressed here is far from dominant. In most countries there are laws against hard-core pornography and "public indecency." Whether there should be such laws, of course, is a question. But let's turn to another principle.

B The benefit to others principle

Imagine Bill Bully throws a rock at Little Liam. Assume Bill wrongfully sets back Liam's interest in not having rocks hit his person. The harm principle thus allows us to interfere with Bill's acts. They need not be tolerated. Now imagine that Little Liam is walking in a park and stubs his toe on a rock. The rock hit his person. Of course, no harm was done – there is no one present to have done a harm (assume it wasn't "planted" there by someone in order to make Liam stub his toe). The harm principle is thus not invoked. Some people would say that the government – or someone – ought nonetheless help Liam and others by removing any rocks that would cause them to have their interests set back in this way. Such people – there are many – may want to end toleration in cases where doing so can benefit individuals even where no one is doing harm. Of course, they don't advocate the absurd – interfering with the rocks as if the rocks had plans. Rather, they advocate interfering to collect monies (perhaps via taxation) to pay for the moving of rocks (perhaps paving) in order to help people like Liam. Putting this differently, there is opposition to a world wherein people like Liam get hurt, and suggestions about interfering to remedy that opposed situation. More often, of course, there is a claim that we ought to collect taxes to alleviate poverty. We interfere, then, with a system that includes poverty, which is opposed.

Toleration, conceptually, can only occur when there is something disliked or disapproved of. Since interference to help those in need takes place without anything being disliked or disapproved of, we are told, failure to interfere designed to help those in need cannot be a case of toleration. I find this a puzzling view for what should be a simple reason: if there were nothing opposed, no one would seek to interfere! It is clear what is opposed: people being in need. More to the point, most of us dislike – and perhaps morally disapprove of – people living in poverty (or people *unnecessarily* living in poverty). In my view, not at least disliking poverty would be a sign of moral depravity. Of course we oppose poverty! This opens the question "should we tolerate people living in poverty or not?" (Tolerating Marvin and tolerating Marvin's starving are not the same; we can oppose people starving without opposing the people.) My view about this is, as I've already indicated (see the Introduction, section B), not mainstream: many political philosophers I have spoken with – and even an anonymous referee of this book – think the language here is too strained. Yet, I think we sometimes talk colloquially of tolerating crime, poverty, and all manner of social ills, and philosophers certainly talk of tolerating social practices (for example, see Wall 2003: 232), and it is, after all, social practices that are generally responsible for poverty in our society (and, arguably, everywhere).

Many liberal theorists, especially in the developed contemporary West, believe that benefiting those in poverty is a good prima facie reason to interfere with the status quo, even where those in poverty cannot be said to be in poverty because of any harm.[3] There must, of course, be interference with *the thing not approved of* if this is to be understood as a limit of toleration. Indeed, the intended object of interference (and non-toleration) is the poverty – which is opposed.[4] Admittedly, this likely involves interference with many others who are neither opposed nor benefited by the interference – those who are taxed to pay for antipoverty programs. (Not interfering with them would also not be toleration, since we do not oppose them.) The point of such a principle, though, is not to determine whether to tolerate behavior of those who have what they need, nor even to determine whether to tolerate the behavior of those who do not have what they need; the point is to determine whether to tolerate poverty.

Whether a benefit to others principle is *a principle of toleration* is an important question. If it is conceived of as providing reason to end toleration – as above – it is. But it may be conceived of quite differently, as a principle of justice at a higher level of theory. This is the case, for example, in both Marxian socialism and Rawlsian liberalism. Neither takes a benefit to others principle as a principle that applies *within* a just society. They take it, rather, as a principle that determines whether a society is just – as a principle used to judge the society from the outside, as it were. Amongst political philosophers, this is actually the more likely use of such a principle.

According to Karl Marx's brand of socialism, the ideal society has no government but is arranged, through voluntary efforts of all residents, in such a way that all those who are capable of contributing do so, and all those who have needs have those needs met. "From each according to his ability, to each according to his needs" (Marx 2001[1875]: 27). That view is not discussed in terms of toleration for a simple reason. There is no interference – nor intentional noninterference – to be discussed. In the socialist utopia that Marx envisions, everyone would seek to do that which is in the interest of everyone else. No interference is needed because, having been re-socialized (after the proletariat revolution and before the utopia emerges), everyone wants to be sure everyone else is OK. In such a utopian state (with the means to produce all that people need), we would not talk of tolerating or failing to tolerate poverty, because there would be no poverty and there would be no government to tolerate or fail to tolerate poverty. Of course, if there is poverty we could talk of individuals tolerating or failing to tolerate poverty. Those who tolerate it would be those who oppose it but for some principled reason intentionally refrain from interfering with it. While some might not interfere merely because they do not oppose the poverty, others might fail to tolerate it because they actively interfere, trying to alleviate poverty.

From *Theory of Justice* forward, John Rawls endorses what he calls "the difference principle," according to which a just society could only have inequalities that work to the advantage of the least well-off. Any society with other inequalities would be (to that extent) unjust. This view does not (immediately) advocate redistributing from the well-off to the less well-off. It suggests, rather, that inequalities in a society can themselves be mechanisms that aid the less well-off. For a simple example, a society wherein medical doctors can accumulate more than others is a society in which there is an incentive for people to become medical doctors – so such a society is likely to be one where the less well-off are more likely to be able to afford good medical care than a more egalitarian society. From outside such a society, there would be no reason to oppose such inequalities – they are good for all, especially those most in need. Hence, from outside such a society, there is no question of toleration (with nothing to oppose).

Utopias aside, it makes perfectly good sense to discuss redistributive policies (policies of taxation and welfare schemes) – in the decidedly non-utopian world you and I occupy – in terms of toleration. We are talking about schemes whereby a government entity taxes some in order to help others by providing them with welfare benefits. Liberals who endorse such a scheme believe that the provision of significant benefits (perhaps determined by need) to some can justify such actions.[5] Most obviously, then, a benefit to others principle would allow a government to tax some to benefit those less well-off in order to alleviate – interfere with – poverty. While such a principle, fully fleshed out, would presumably limit the sorts and amounts of permitted interferences, it provides justification for redistribution of resources to help specific individuals. Just as some liberals (libertarians) favor the harm principle as the only normative principle of toleration, and some (Feinberg) prefer to include the offense principle, so others endorse the benefit to others principle.

Many believe that there is a moral problem with the benefit to others principle as a principle of toleration *within a system* because it would require that the government interfere with some in order to help others – so even if it is, conceptually, a matter of toleration (of poverty rather than people), it requires *wrongful interference with some people (taxpayers) using their money as they see fit*. That is, we would fail to tolerate their use of money to purchase everyday, mundane items like books, electronic equipment, food, children's toys, schooling, etc. (At least, it's a failure to tolerate if we oppose them having as much as they do or using their money as they see fit. This, though, is not the point here.) I am sympathetic to this objection, but it is important to remember that the point of a benefit to others principle is that it allows an end to toleration to aid those in poverty (so refuses to tolerate poverty).[6] What is tolerated or not in government redistribution programs is poverty. We might refuse to tolerate here because we oppose people living in poverty and value everyone being able to lead good, or at least decent, lives. That is, we intentionally interfere with something we dislike or disapprove of on principle. This is, I hope it is clear, an admirable goal. Poverty is bad; alleviating it is good. Moreover, the objection assumes, without argument, that the only way to fail to tolerate poverty is to interfere by taking from those who have much. There is reason to doubt this, as we will see.

Of course, it is possible that some will insist we should tolerate poverty – refrain from interfering with the opposed thing (poverty) because of a commitment, perhaps, to individual liberty of those who would otherwise be interfered with (primarily those with much, but conceivably also those with little). But others will simply disapprove of a social system in its entirety if it is such that it allows some to be impoverished. Such people may believe it right to intentionally not refrain from interfering – in order to prevent the continuation of that sort of system, which they oppose. That is, they will think we ought not tolerate the system as a whole. It is a system, after all, in which some are allowed (or perhaps even caused) to live in poverty. Such a system should be opposed. We can all agree that a system where no one lives in poverty – even if some are worse off than others – is better than one wherein some do, all other things equal. The principle that this is a prima facie good reason to end toleration is a form of benefit to others principle.

Given the atrocious living conditions of many in poverty, there is a clear intuition in favor of benefiting others. No good person wants others to suffer (perhaps excepting others who committed heinous crimes). Still, we should admit that a state that accepts the benefit to others principle will put limits on some of its residents. It interferes with their spending and thus limits their ability to do as they wish. Harold wants to buy his children new bicycles, but the money he planned to use for that purpose is confiscated in order to pay for food for those who are less well-off. Great for the less well-off. Not so great for Harold or his children.

This is too simple though. Perhaps less money is taken to aid the less well-off. In this more moderate system, Harold still can't buy his children new bikes, but he buys them used bikes. Joe Poor gets the food he needs. Harold's children get bikes. We should, though, look further than these obvious and good effects to the generally unseen costs, including the opportunity costs of the interference with Harold – whether the higher or lower taxation. Say the interference (taxation) had not taken place. Harold buys his children new bikes. He buys them from a store. The store, in turn, is doing a greater business than anticipated and needs to hire an extra employee. They hire Joe Poor. Joe is not (as) poor now. He can buy the food he needs that would, in the first system, be given to him and potentially discourage him from looking for work. Without the interference, there is greater incentive to seek gainful employment, greater ability of the less well-off to buy what they need for themselves, and fewer limits on the abilities of those like Harold to do as they please. This is admittedly much too quick (see Schmidtz and Goodin 1998 for a lengthier treatment). Still, it makes clear (I hope) that when considering interference with others, we should be mindful of the incentives we set up and the opportunity costs we impose. In my own view, when we are mindful of these factors we are less likely to interfere with others. Sometimes that noninterference will be toleration and sometimes it will not. The benefit to others principle, to my mind, encourages too much interference – and in part does so because it fails to take these things into consideration.[7]

Importantly, even the harm principle alone will allow interference to alleviate poverty when the poverty is itself a harm caused by some particular agents. If agent A harms agent B, agent A can be interfered with according to the harm principle. If Alex steals Bridgette's car and so causes her to lose her job, he can be interfered with – and, I should think, must compensate her, perhaps even for her lost wages.

Importantly, agent A might not intend to harm B, but might nonetheless culpably engage in an activity that results in B having interests set back – and the fact that A was culpably involved matters. So, for example, if you buy an iPhone on the "five finger market" and it turns out that the iPhone in question was mine, you have culpably engaged in an activity – theft and black market purchase of stolen goods – that leaves me with my interests wrongfully set back. You are culpable – and so can be said to participate in the harm to me – because you should have known not to buy an iPhone where you did. You may not have harmed me on your own, but you did participate in a system that harmed me. Talk of punishment here may make little sense. In such a case, the warranted interference might be some sort of restitution or reparation. Given that you were not solely responsible, you may not have to pay the full restitution on your own. It may be that there should be some sort of systemic assistance program meant to compensate those who suffer harms (genuine harms, not mere hurts) attributable to many agents, though not all individually identifiable. This becomes more plausible as larger and larger groups cause the harms in question. I will discuss this sort of issue in the international arena more extensively in chapter 5B, but assume something similar can happen domestically. It has not, of course, been the focus of discussions about the alleviation of poverty.

C　The principle of legal paternalism

If one advocates the strict version of the harm principle, one believes that interference – lack of toleration – is only permitted when someone is about to harm, is harming, or has harmed another. Some people, though, often say things indicating they think the government or others should interfere with an individual acting in ways that affect no one else. They suggest, for example, that "there ought to be a law" against riding a bike without a helmet, running with scissors, or hiring an unlicensed hair stylist to cut one's hair. There are actually laws in a variety of places of the first and third type, just as there are laws against a variety of drugs. These are all paternalistic laws: laws that disallow toleration of activities that could cause the actor herself to have some interest set back.[8] In common parlance, we'd say they are laws against *harming oneself*. According to the paternalist, interference (rather than toleration) is prima facie justified if needed to prevent individuals from causing themselves harm. I reject this view, but indicate limits to that rejection and note its widespread endorsement in law. Of course, some readers may disagree and think this principle should be defended.

In chapter 3D, we saw reason to think legal paternalism is problematic: there is difficulty with the very idea of wronging oneself and the sense of harm relevant to the harm principle requires (conceptually) a wrong. Nonetheless, as also suggested, that is only an issue when the individual is fully rational. Hence, many advocate *soft paternalism*. On this view, interference is justified to ensure that when an individual acts in such a way that will cause her hurt, she does so rationally and fully cognizant of the likely consequences. For example, if Betty is about to walk across a dilapidated bridge, we are fully warranted (some might even think required) in asking her if she realizes there is danger. She may not, of course, and would then likely thank us for the warning. This is not interference; it is rational dialogue, which, as indicated in chapter 3E, is always permitted and fully consistent with toleration. The only way this becomes problematic is if we must physically prevent Betty from crossing the bridge in order to engage in the dialogue (and then it's physical

intervention followed by rational dialogue). Such intervention is permissible on the soft paternalist view, so long as the
intent is only to guarantee that the agent interfered with is
"in her right mind" and understands the consequences of her
actions. Further physical intervention and coercion are not
permitted (hence this view is also sometimes called *soft
anti-paternalism*).

We should admit that there will be times when determining
if someone is in her right mind will be difficult. There may
be, obviously, language barriers. In such cases, it seems reasonable to physically intervene until a translator is available.
In other cases, we may have no language barrier but find
ourselves unable to believe anyone could rationally want
what the person says they want. Consider Donald "Dax"
Cowart.[9] Dax was burned badly – with 65 percent of his
body severely affected, much with third-degree burns – and
was rushed to the hospital. He was hospitalized for more than
a year and consistently insisted that treatment be halted and
that he be allowed to die. The doctors did not know, when
he first arrived, if they could save him. They were unable to
alleviate all his pain. In my view, Dax should have been
allowed to die, to take his own life, to be given assistance in
taking his own life, and even to be the patient of euthanasia.[10]
That is, these options should have been tolerated, since no
one else would have been harmed. Of course, in endorsing
the soft paternalist perspective, I would first insist that a
psychologist (or two) be allowed to talk with Dax to determine whether he is sane enough to make the decision.
Importantly, though, this has to be a real option.

Some may insist that anyone who wants to kill himself
must be "crazy," but there is little evidence for that view.
Let's make the Dax case even worse than it was. Call this
the RUDy Case (for "Really Unfortunate Dax-like"). RUDy
is in exactly the same situation as Dax in terms of the burns
and the available medical care, but there is more going on.
His parents died two years before the accident that caused
his burns and his wife left him a week before it. RUDy's
daughter is in jail for murdering an innocent child and RUDy
knows she is guilty and unrepentant. RUDy's son is a drug
addict and a pedophile whom RUDy himself turned in to
the police since, again, he knows he is guilty. Moreover,

RUDy was fired for incompetence from the job he held for 15 years and that he loved. His life, in short, is in shambles. He has tried reconciling with his wife but she wants nothing to do with him. He has tried to help his children and they have completely rebuffed him. Before the accident, RUDy had been trying to determine how to kill himself. He had set in his mind, quite firmly, that he would do so within a month and was only waiting to determine how best to do the deed. Then the accident happened. It really was not his doing, but when it first occurred, his only thought was "Thank you God for making this easier!" Then the ambulance came, dashing his hopes.

It seems clear that RUDy is in a situation where it would be quite reasonable to seek an exit. It's not clear to me what someone trying to persuade him to live could say. One might start with: "Your friends will miss you." He might consider this and truthfully respond: "My friends were either friends of my wife or friends from work; the former all let me know they would not speak with me since they prefer her to me; the latter have all let me know that they are very pleased they don't have to work with me anymore. I was obviously a bad person, though I didn't know it at the time; either that or I was a bad judge of character and all the people I associated with are worse than I thought." One might try to respond: "But you can make new friends, get a new job, and gain much!" RUDy might think about this and truthfully respond: "You are right, but it would require much effort I don't want to expend; I didn't want to last week and I don't want to now. I want out." What more can be said?

Some will insist, perhaps for religious reasons, that suicide is immoral. I'll consider that issue in the next section. Here, though, the only issue is whether RUDy's hurting himself warrants interference beyond that required to determine if he is in his right mind when choosing death. Given the description of the case, I think the answer is clear. Granted that his sanity is intact, his hurting himself would be *his* choice so, by *Volenti*, the harm principle does not permit interference. Those who think the interference is permitted would knowingly require RUDy to live in physical and emotional pain. Indeed, in my view, RUDy's ending his life is not even a hurt – it is the reduction of hurt.

Still, there might be some who endorse *hard paternalism* – the view that interference is permitted to prevent an individual from hurting herself even when she rationally endorses her action – and who would allow that in cases like RUDy's interference is not permitted. They might, that is, endorse some form of hard paternalism that allows coercive or forceful interference in some cases, but not cases like RUDy's (or even Dax's). Their paternalism may be a genuine interest in protecting others, and they may accept that interfering with RUDy (or Dax) does not in any way protect him – it leaves him in pain.

This seems like a reasonable approach at first. And indeed, defenders of hard paternalism often suggest that they would not defend interference in all cases where an agent is acting in a way that will knowingly hurt only him. They claim that they would only interfere after considering the merits of the case.[11] If the hurt that would be caused is significant, long term, or intense, that counts in favor of interference on their view. If the hurt is minor, short term, and recoverable, or easily bearable, that counts against interference. Such thinkers usually also indicate that if the agent in question appears to be underestimating the risk, that counts in favor of interference. None of this seems to me an adequate defense.

The idea that the agent might be underestimating the risk, in my view, should be considered as part of the process of determining the rationality and competence of the agent. If she is really incapable of estimating the risk properly, the soft paternalist would agree to the interference. The other ideas strike me as unhelpful. Is RUDy's death worse than or better than his continued existence in pain? Does the long-term contentness he may have found years after being released from the hospital outweigh the short-term existence in intense pain? Inevitably, in all these cases, what is being suggested is that the person (or agency) who is considering interfering should substitute their judgment of the situation for the patient's. The paternalist basically says, "There is no way he could want what he says he wants," and what this means, in effect, is "There is no way *I* could want what he says he wants." Similarly, the hospital in Dax's case decided his life was worth more than the pain he was suffering – though he clearly disagreed.

As I indicated at the beginning of this section, some readers may think there are cases where hard paternalism is appropriate. If so, they should be prepared to defend some principled basis for the sorts of judgments that I indicate in the last paragraph are needed. I cannot say that this is impossible, but I am skeptical. Of course, most governments retain paternalist laws. Laws against riding a motorcycle without a helmet, against drug use, against fireworks, requiring prescriptions for medications, requiring licenses for doctors, hairdressers, etc.: these are all justified – supposedly – by the need to protect those who would otherwise hurt themselves.[12] I do not list these to defend paternalism – so far as I can tell, the existence of a law for X is poor evidence that X is good. I would say the arguments against paternalism are arguments against such laws. We have two mutually inconsistent views: (hard) paternalism and its rejection. I accept the latter.

Given its recent popularity, I should briefly discuss what is called "libertarian paternalism." This might seem like an oxymoron: the libertarian endorses the strict version of the harm principle and so rejects paternalism, so one can't be a libertarian paternalist. However, according to defenders of this view,[13] the state can make laws in ways designed to encourage people not to hurt themselves – indeed, to help themselves – while tolerating them doing the opposite. Laws like this are thought not to involve interference as they involve the use only of *defaults* that can be chosen against. Some might think that default-setting is itself interference, but there must be defaults and this sort of interference – if interference it be – cannot reasonably be considered coercive. More to the point, so long as the default is set in a way such that people could opt out without bearing any significant cost – that is, without being interfered with in any serious way – there doesn't seem to be any problem with toleration. That is, all would be tolerated.

Consider an example. Say that the default is that nothing is taken out of your paycheck but you are encouraged to invest for your retirement with an option of having 10 percent of your paycheck directly deposited in a retirement account for you. Now say that the legal default is that 10 percent of your salary is always taken out of your pay and put in a retirement account that you will be able to access once you turn 65. This is a default only, though. Just as in the first case, where you have an option to use a payroll deduction for retirement savings, in this case you have an option not to. You are free to sign a form saying you want that money left in your paycheck. Your decision would be accepted and the behavior (not putting money in that sort of account) tolerated. It does not seem that either of these possibilities is a problem. The latter possibility is paternalist in that its justification is to encourage the employee to act in a way that will leave her with resources when she retires. However, the law is designed to tolerate those who wish not to participate (preserving freedom) by allowing them to opt out, signing a waver so that they receive their full pay, forgoing the otherwise imposed retirement savings plan.

Still, it is likely that state-enforced changes to defaults require extra care in their institution in order to not cause harm. For example, assume the law currently requires that, when an employer pays an employee, 10 percent is withdrawn from the latter's pay and automatically deposited into an account that is inaccessible until retirement – and that the employee has no say in the matter. Everyone in the society is used to this system and so no one worries about saving for their retirement. In moving from such a system to a paternalist libertarian system where people could opt out, care must be taken to be sure that anyone wishing to opt out fully understands what they are losing. (If this is successful, a further step might be possible wherein the default was no automatic savings but an option for such a plan is offered. To move from the current system to such a system directly seems too risky.)

D   The principle of legal moralism

Finally, we come to legal moralism. According to the moralist, interference is prima facie justified if needed to prevent some immoralities, even where these cause no harms. This, I will argue, should be simply and definitively rejected – even though it, like paternalism, continues to play a role in the law of most countries, including those that appear to be the most liberal. Of course, some readers may disagree.

Politically influential thinkers have advocated this principle. In the UK in the 1950s and 1960s, the famed jurist Sir Patrick Devlin argued that homosexuality should remain illegal on the grounds that it is immoral and such immoralities tear at the fabric of society.[14] Devlin (1968) seemed to think that this "harm to society" resulted in harms also to the individuals living in the society – who presumably needed a "healthy society" to be healthy themselves. Others have held that such harm to individuals is at best a side issue and that interference is permissible even to prevent "free-floating evils" – immoralities that cause no harm at all (see Feinberg 1990: 3–38, 124–75; Hart 1963: 48–52). More recently, the US Supreme Court upheld something very like Devlin's view in *Bowers v. Hardwick* (1986). That decision was overturned in *Lawrence v. Texas* (2003), but a dissenting opinion in that case repeated the Devlin view.

There are really (at least) three views that can be considered versions of legal moralism. First, the view I attribute to Devlin: harmless immoralities are not really harmless since, although no one is directly harmed by the action in question, it somehow harms society as a whole and that ends up harming individuals in the society. Call this "Devlin's social impact moralism." Second, the view attributed to James Fitzjames Stephen, the Victorian jurisprudence scholar, in his response to Mill: harmless immoralities harm society as a whole whether or not they harm any individual directly or indirectly. Call this "Stephen's societal harm moralism."[15] Finally, the view that some things are simply immoral and must be interfered with for that reason alone, even if no individual is hurt and society itself is not hurt. Call this "free-floating evils moralism." (I ordered these views from most to least plausible.)

Now let's consider the Dax case introduced in the last section. In particular, let us ask whether legal moralism in any of the three forms just delineated would offer a plausible reason to interfere in Dax's (or RUDy's) suicide. According to Devlin's social impact moralism, if it is to be interfered with, Dax's suicide would have to hurt society in such a way that others ended up suffering. According to Stephen's societal harm moralism, it would only have to hurt society. Finally, according to free-floating evils moralism, no one and no society needs to be hurt; it just needs to be so evil that it merits interference. The first two are simply implausible. The case is so extreme and rare that to think that it would in some way harm society as a whole to allow Dax to kill himself just seems unbelievable, perhaps relying on an implausible slippery slope claim that allowing one person to commit suicide would result in many people taking their own lives. (The evidence from societies wherein euthanasia is legal suggests no reason to worry.) Of course, other cases will not be as extreme. But first consider the third sort of moralism. Is Dax's suicide so evil that it should be interfered with? As I indicated in chapter 3C, I do think there are objective facts about moral issues. Nonetheless, I can't here offer further defense of the claim (that I believe) that it is objectively *not* immoral for Dax to kill himself, for someone to help him do so, or to mercifully kill him upon his request. I think it's more important, at this point, to simply indicate that we would need an argument that these things are immoral if we adopt the principle of moralism and think toleration of Dax is not required. That is, we need a two-part argument showing (1) that Dax's suicide would be immoral and (2) that immorality makes it worth disallowing even at the cost of keeping Dax alive in pain, against his wishes. Absent such an argument, the claim that his – and especially RUDy's – suicide should not be tolerated simply strikes me as sadistic. That is, not only is there no free-floating evil here, there is likely a good *for Dax*.

The Dax case is extreme and so may not be the best sort of example to consider here. So, what sort of acts would be *evil enough without causing harm* to merit interference?

Of course, we are not discussing natural evils like hurricanes, etc. Just as these cannot wrong a person and so cannot harm a person, they cannot be immoral in any sense relevant to this discussion. A tornado does not intend to wreak havoc. A tornado does not intend anything. To hold it morally responsible – or to say it is acting immorally – is to make what we call a category mistake. It is to treat something as if it belongs in a category it does not. A university, for example, is not (or not merely) a set of buildings, and to treat it as if it were is to make a category mistake. Similarly, to treat a tornado as if it could be morally blameworthy is to make a category mistake, treating it as a moral agent when it is not.

What we are talking about here are what Feinberg calls "non-grievance evils" (see 1990: 17–20). These are morally bad things that no one can justifiably claim to be wronged by and so that supply no one with a legitimate grievance even though the acts are nonetheless wrong. Feinberg distinguishes two sorts of non-grievance evils: "welfare-connected evils" and "free-floating evils." The former are immoralities that leave some individuals less well-off even though they have no legitimate grievance. These are clearly relevant for Devlin's view. Free-floating evils, by contrast, have no impact on anyone's interests – they are of concern, obviously, in free-floating evils moralism. People have thought that taboo sexual relations (like fully consensual incest), extramarital sexual activity of those in consensually open relationships, homosexuality, masturbation, exploitation, and acts that contribute to the corruption of a person (or their soul) are free-floating evils. We can't discuss all of these.

The obvious sorts of cases to consider here, I think, are cases of pornography and homosexuality (I think neither is immoral, but legal moralists often do). For now, I simply note that these are actually widespread in our society and our society doesn't seem hurt in any significant way. (Some religious fanatics claimed 9/11 was a punishment for our society's immorality, but I assume my readers do not take such views seriously. No being reasonably called "God" – that is, no all-good being – would want to hurt innocent people as a response to purported moral problems in the societies they inhabit.) It's also important that there is no good argument that homosexuality is immoral, and that the better arguments about pornography being immoral are limited in their conclusions (perhaps concluding that pornography is immoral *if* it helps sustain a culture wherein women are treated as of less value than men). So let's consider a different sort of case.

Consider, briefly, Patrick Stuebing and Susan Karolewski. Patrick and Susan are biological siblings, but their parents divorced when they were very young and they only met again when he was 23 and she was a teenager. They fell in love and had children. Leaving aside the possible health issues they may impose on their children, should their relationship be tolerated? According to a standard moralist, it should not. Let's consider the three sorts of moralism.

The Devlin social impact moralist position here would be something close to Devlin's own view about homosexuality: if it is tolerated, society will suffer – perhaps because of a "tearing" of the social fabric that leaves people within the society (fabric) less "connected" and in that way suffering a loss to their welfare (the marriage would be a welfare-connected evil). When faced with this sort of claim, I think it is important to ask why the "fabric of society" would be torn – that is, why would people be less connected? The answer, so far as I can tell, is simply that knowledge of the relationship would cause offense to some who would then seek distance from those who offend. If my diagnosis is correct, though, this is an issue for those who endorse the offense principle, not moralism. Stating that differently, this is an issue that might encourage endorsement of the offense principle, not legal moralism. But before endorsing that principle because of cases like this, one should realize that refusing to tolerate the fully consensual relationship between Patrick and Susan because others may react poorly is off-putting, to say the least. After all, many worried about giving women and African Americans equal rights because some (white men) might react poorly. It was a poor defense of a failure of toleration then and it's a poor defense now. Sometimes people have their welfare set back by things that should not affect them at all – and those are often things we should tolerate.

What of Stephen's societal harm moralism? Is society itself harmed by Patrick and Susan's love and potential marriage? My response to this is not dependent on the case. As that view is described above, it is entirely about harms to society itself and, in my view, there simply is *no such thing that can be harmed*. Society is nothing more than a collection of individuals living together (loosely speaking), under some set of rules, both explicit and implicit. The individuals can be hurt or harmed. They have interests that can be set back. The collection, though, has no interests to be set back. The rules that govern the interactions of those in society may themselves be set back in the sense that fewer people may abide by them, but if this is a problem, it is a problem because of what it does to the individuals – not because of the collection or the rules themselves. Imagine, for comparison, a set of metal marbles held in place by the presence of a magnet. Weakening the magnet (the rules or rule-setting device) weakens the connection of the marbles, but not the marbles. Someone might be upset that the marbles are no longer in order, but this would be a setback to that person's interests, not the interests of the set of marbles. The set of marbles has no interests. Nor does a set of persons, even though each person (unlike each marble) in the set does have interests and may share numerous interests with the others. Hence, Patrick and Susan's relationship does not set back the interests of society – for there are no such interests. If anyone has their interests set back it is some set of individuals. That, of course, may be a reason for interference – if the setback is also wrongful and thus harmful. But that would be an issue for the harm principle, not legal moralism. (Or if it's an issue for legal moralism, its Devlin's social impact moralism, which we've already discussed.)

What about free-floating evils moralism? Again, while I am not prepared to offer a complete defense of the claim that there is no immorality in Patrick and Susan's union, it is important to realize that we would need an argument to this effect. That is, we need a two-part argument showing (1) that their relationship is immoral and (2) that that immorality *alone* makes it worth disallowing even at the cost of hurting Patrick and Susan (and their children). I can think of only one plausible argument:[16] that the union is immoral because it wrongfully causes children to be born into a harmed or harmful situation because of their genetic code. But then we again invoke the harm principle, and legal moralism is irrelevant. Notice also that a romantic relationship does not have to result in the birth of children at all, so it is not the relationship itself that should be disallowed if it is harm that matters, but only (if anything) the biological creation of children in that relationship.

Contemporary liberals have consistently rejected legal moralism, for good reason (Hart 1963; Feinberg 1990). Moralistic legislation detracts too much from individuals being able to act on their autonomous choices (or choices consistent with their consciences) – something important for a number of reasons. First, as Mill argues (chapter 3 of *On Liberty*; see chapter 7B and D below),[17] the ability to act on one's own choices is important as doing so allows one to develop one's reasoning abilities. Moreover, as rationality is often seen as a defining characteristic of personhood or humanity, choice is instrumentally valuable for maintaining (and increasing) one's humanity (certainly it is seen this way by Mill). Second, the fact is that we have more intimate knowledge, generally speaking, of our projects than others do,[18] and so are more likely to achieve our projects when we are free to choose what we do (see chapter 7F). Choice, then, is instrumentally valuable to the satisfaction of projects. Third, Mill claims that freedom to choose how one leads one's life is necessary in order to allow for the existence of genius and societal progress (see Mill 1978[1859]: 61–7; also see chapter 7G below). Geniuses are unique, having unusual talents. If they are forced to do as others insist, their creativity is likely to be stifled and that would lessen the innovation and progress available in society. Put more simply, if no one is permitted to choose against societal norms, no one would come up with new – and possibly better – ways of doing things. Choice, then, is instrumentally valuable as a means to innovation and progress. By allowing individuals to choose on their own, we allow them the opportunity to develop new and better ways of performing daily tasks and to develop new and better ways of life. Indeed, while legal moralism may sound appealing to politically conservative pundits, it is also conservative in the original sense of that word. It seeks to conserve the currently existing order *merely for the sake of conserving the currently existing order*. I suggest, by contrast, that if there is something valuable in a social order, it can be defended, but that merely defending some way of being because it is *our* way of being will not do. That would be a recipe for stagnation. Finally, choice is also intrinsically valuable. We can see this by asking ourselves about the following scenario. Say you are planning on waking up on Saturday and going to play ball at the park with friends. You wake up, shower, dress, eat, and leave the house. As you are about to get in your car with your sports equipment, you black out. Someone has put chloroform on you. When you wake, you are standing at the park you were planning to go to, with your sports equipment, by your car. You are confused. Do you think, "Oh well, I am where I wanted to be, so all is well," or "Who the hell brought me here? They had no right to do that!" If you think the latter, though none of your interests (other than the interest in acting on your own volition) has been set back – they have in fact been forwarded (you are where you wanted to be, after all, and perhaps earlier than you would have managed on your own) – you think there is some non-instrumental value in acting on your own choice. You think, that is, that choice is intrinsically valuable. Given the tremendous value of acting on your own choice, a weighty case would be needed to justify overriding that ability.

This chapter is largely about political and legal morality, but would be incomplete without some mention of interpersonal morality (or interpersonal moral relationships). Indeed, much of what I have said about these principles and what sorts of interferences they would allow by the state applies, mutatis mutandis, to individuals. Regarding moralism, I should note that I take it to be completely uncontroversial that people should be moral. Of course, what it means for people to be moral is controversial. As should be clear from the discussion of harmless immoralities, many of us believe there are more ways to be immoral than to harm someone. If that is the case (I think it is),[19] we will sometimes – perhaps even often – tolerate immorality if we reject moralism. Of course, since toleration is consistent with rational persuasion, we can – and should – try to persuade those considering moral wrongdoing not to act in that fashion. Force and coercion (lack of toleration), though, should only be used in cases of harms – a particular class of immoral acts.

E   More hard cases

I suspect that readers of this work will be antecedently inclined to oppose both paternalism and moralism, and perhaps also the offense principle. I assume most readers will think the Chinese court was wrong, for example, when it

sentenced Ma Yaohai, a 53-year-old computer science profes-
sor, to three and a half years in jail for hosting and participat-
ing in orgies and partner swapping (see Edward Wong, "18
Orgies Later, Chinese Swinger Gets Prison Bed," *New York
Times*, May 20, 2010). Most will likely think that what Mr.
Ma does in his own time, with consenting partners, is his own
business, whether or not they think his actions offensive or
immoral and whether or not they think he is hurting himself.
To combat this complacency, it is important to push the
intuitions behind the principles with examples that many
people take to be beyond the pale. Indeed, we have discussed
several in the process of discussing the various possible principles of toleration. Three more cases might be especially
compelling.

The first case is the 2002 German case of Armin Meiwes.
Mr. Meiwes advertised for a homosexual male to engage in
a fairly gruesome activity. Meiwes planned to butcher the
volunteer and eat him. Interestingly, it appears that several
individuals had previously responded to the ad and met with
Meiwes, even allowing themselves to be readied for slaughter,
and that when they decided, just before being cut, that they
did not want to go through with it, Meiwes let them go (see
Berry-Dee and Morris 2010: 24). Meiwes nonetheless was
able to carry through his gruesome desire, actually sharing
the first meal – his victim's sex organ – after Bernd Jürgen
Brandes responded to the ad.[20] Brandes was then butchered
and killed. Many of us assume that Brandes must have been
in some way psychologically incapacitated, rendering the
Volenti principle mute so that Meiwes is guilty of violating
the harm principle. I suspect that is right, but if it is not – if
Brandes was in his right mind and did consent – some will
nonetheless insist that interference, and not toleration, is warranted. This would be due to paternalism (for Brandes, presumably), moralism (against the whole act), or offense (again,
against the whole act). To adopt the strict version of the harm
principle, by contrast, is to deny that interference is justified
if Brandes was in his right mind.

Consider also the US case of Sharon Lopatka in 1996.
Lopatka, who we might also suspect needed psychological
counseling, left her husband, leaving him a note asking him
"not to pursue the person who would kill her" and noting

that even if her body was never recovered, he should know she was "at peace." She had met a man in an online chatroom with whom she had exchanged more than 100 email messages. In their chat and correspondence, he promised to sexually torture and kill her; more than one person in the chat room "tried to convince her not to act on her deathwish." She apparently went through with it; her body was found two weeks later (see McConnell 2000, 8–9; Cohen 2007: 491ff).

It is important that in both the cases just discussed, we are likely to suspect that some form of psychological problem is present. Our suspicion, though, is not much more than that. One can imagine, I think, certain sorts of individuals rationally choosing to be the sort of victims (if that is what they are) in those examples. Indeed, the final case to consider here makes this perfectly clear.

The final case concerns the contemporary performance artist Marina Abramovic. In one of her early works, Abramovic lay naked on a table with various instruments – including a saw, a gun, and a bullet – surrounding her. People would walk around her and were able to use the instruments in whichever way they chose – sometimes inflicting wounds on her (some also became protectors, stopping others from engaging in hurtful behavior).[21] I suspect this sort of activity would be interfered with in many places, including the US. (The piece was executed in Naples.) While some may have doubted her sanity at the time, the 30-plus years of work she has done since seem to clearly demonstrate that this early work was part of a rich artistic project, voluntarily chosen and enacted. Hence, if interference is permitted, it cannot be because of the harm principle. It might be because of the offense principle, but it would be more likely opposed by those endorsing legal moralism or legal paternalism.

Consider these cases. If we reject the offense principle and legal paternalism and moralism, as I suggest we should, toleration is mandated in all three if all involved were fully sane. If Brandes was in his right mind – perhaps counterfactually – and aware of the consequences of his consent – as he must have been – his activity with Meiwes must be tolerated. The same holds for Lopatka. Similarly, Abramovic's art must be tolerated if we reject those three principles, though it often left her in an extremely dangerous position. I think these are the right conclusions, but I may be wrong. The reader should not accept my view without considering these sorts of cases carefully and determining whether an argument in defense of the intuition that the acts should be banned can be mounted.

Here's a concession – and a challenge: I share the intuition that the acts should be banned. They are, in my personal opinion, beyond the pale (especially the Meiwes case). But my personal opinion is no more at issue here than yours, Dear Reader. What is at issue are the arguments. I would be happy to hear a compelling argument defending the intuition for limiting toleration in these cases. Absent such an argument, though, I am unwilling to rest with an intuition – even my own. So, is there such an argument? If you have one, please share it!

5
Extending the Harm Principle

While Mill argues that two or more people can consent to an activity that would otherwise be considered harmful and thus render it harmless (though not hurtless), his discussion is largely confined to adult individuals in a single cultural group. Indeed, some of what he says elsewhere about interference internationally (and interculturally) rightly appalls liberals today. He nonetheless provides us with the tools to go further. In this chapter, I will explain how the harm principle can be used to discuss what should be tolerated regarding animals and the environment, between cultural groups within one's country and internationally, and of corporate groups and other actors in the business world.

A The environment and animals

First, it is worth considering nonhuman animals and the environment. Many today want to defend both of these as having independent intrinsic value. There is no reason here to dispute this claim, though I tend to doubt the environment has intrinsic value.[1] Thinking that animals, on the other hand, have value on their own, seems quite plausible. To see this, one need only recognize that animals act in many ways like humans do. Baby puppies seek comfort from their mother.

Elephants even make pilgrimages to sites where there are bones of their ancestors (i.e., burial grounds). Perhaps it's anthropomorphizing the animals, but absent a more fitting explanation for why they act in this way, I suggest we do better to think of these sorts of behaviors as common to a class of creatures larger than that of humanity alone. If this is not persuasive, consider what we would think of someone who took a puppy or a kitten and burned it alive, or "cooked" it in a microwave. Most of us shudder at the thought. Even if we are told it was done as an experiment necessary to cure some disease that inflicts humans, we find it repulsive.[2]

What is important for our purposes is that it is clear that nonhuman animals can and do have interests that can be set back. Their interests are presumably narrower than ours – they do not have an interest, I assume, in living to be a certain age (since they do not understand the concept of age), they do not have an interest in acting autonomously (I assume they have neither the concept nor the ability), and they do not have an interest in acting on their own conscience (I assume they do not have a conscience, in the relevant sense). While some prefer to limit the harm principle to discussions of human persons (Mill likely meant it this way), there is no reason we cannot use it to also discuss other animals, so long as we are clear about the sorts of interests each species can have.

I assume all sentient animals have an interest in not suffering.[3] Torturing kittens, then, sets back their interests and (I assume) does so wrongly, so harms them. The harm principle thus permits an end to toleration (perhaps by individuals, perhaps by the government) so as to allow interference with anyone attempting to engage in such activity. The same can be said for other animals and activities that wrongfully set back their interests. Forcing dogs to fight to the death, keeping baby calves basically immobile to make their meat tastier, and tying up a horse's testicles to make it buck at a rodeo: all plausibly set back the interests of those animals wrongly; if they do so, morally they can be interfered with.

The environment is a different sort of entity from that of kittens, dogs, cows, and horses. Regardless of its value, the environment is not the sort of thing that has interests and so is not the sort of thing that can have interests set back. As such, it cannot be "harmed" as that term is used in the harm principle. Damaging the environment – which is not the same as "hurting" it if we take hurting to be either setting back of interests (as I do throughout) or causing pain (a perfectly reasonable way we use the word) – does not, according to the harm principle, warrant an end to toleration. At least not on its own.

While we can't use the harm principle to directly discuss the environment anymore than we can use it to discuss human artifacts – in both cases because they cannot have interests set back – there is an indirect use of the harm principle that is important here. Consider Paul the paper-mill owner. When Paul dumps chemicals into the river that runs by his mill, those chemicals end up poisoning the fish and land near his downstream neighbors. Economists say Paul creates *negative externalities* that his neighbors must deal with. In our terminology, Paul sets back the interests of those neighbors, forcing *them* to take responsibility for *his* actions, paying some of the costs of his paper production. It seems clear he is acting wrongly; he is making money by milling and selling paper and any profit he earns in the process seems dishonest if he does not pay the full cost of the milling. Just as we would be incensed if he refused to pay his workers, we should be incensed if he refused to compensate those to whom he wrongfully causes a loss (in the current case, we assume it to be wrongful as they did not agree to the activity). The downstream neighbors lose clean water. They lose the ability to fish the stream. They may lose their livelihood. Hence, while we cannot say Paul harms (in the relevant sense) the environment, we can say his treatment of the environment harms his neighbors, just as we could say Peter harms Mary if he breaks her lamp though he does not harm the lamp. The harm principle thus allows us to interfere with Paul's (and Peter's) activities on behalf of those neighbors (or Mary). Similar argumentation applies to oil spills by large corporations (e.g., the British Petroleum spill in the Gulf of Mexico in 2010).

Some may suggest that if I am right so far, I have simply provided reason to think that in the last chapter I must have left out some other principle that would indicate that toleration permissibly ends when the environment is damaged and no persons (like the downstream neighbors) are harmed. They might think the environment is simply so valuable on

its own, regardless of its effects on persons, that we need
something like an "environment protection principle" (EPP).
Or they might think that damaging animals in ways that do
not set back their interests (euthanizing them, for example)
might warrant an end to toleration even though there is no
violation of the harm principle (remember, animals don't
have interests in staying alive) and so insist there must be an
"animal protection principle" (APP). Or they might think we
need some single principle that would cover both protection
of animals as well as protection of the environment, without
consideration of harm. Call it a "principle protecting the
environment and animals" (PPEA).

I am skeptical about the defensibility of an EPP, an APP,
or a PPEA. Absent some worked-out understanding of such
a principle, though, I can't argue directly against it. Some
people attempt to defend the claim that animals have rights
that require something like an APP. While I am dubious of
such a claim, I won't argue against it. I will only say that if
it grants more protections to animals than those that are
provided given the harm principle and their limited interests,
some rather fancy argumentation would be needed. I think
the harm principle gets things right. Beings with interests
should have protection from harms. When their interests are
set back, there is cause for concern. Sometimes, of course,
interests are set back in ways – by hurricanes and tornadoes,
for example – that are not due to any action of anyone who
can be blamed, and in those cases there is no interference
warranted because there is no one to interfere with.[4] However,
when their interests are set back wrongfully – when some
specific moral agent acts in a wrongful way that results in
their interests being set back – then interference is permitted.
Toleration permissibly ends at this point, as indicated by the
harm principle.

B   Domestic cultural groups and the international community

The general approach being advocated here should now be
fairly clear: determine if one agent's action would wrongfully

set back the interests of another; if it would, interference is permissible; otherwise, refrain from interfering. Refraining from interfering is toleration if it is principled and the action is opposed (which it presumably is, if the question arises). This general approach seems to serve us well. Let us consider it in relation to cultural groups and international issues.

First, take differing cultural groups within a single polity – the domestic case. There are two additional important factors here: (1) we are assuming that the domestic society is just and (2) we must know what membership in the relevant cultural groups amounts to. The first of these assumptions is important for a fairly simple reason: if the society in which a cultural group exists is itself just, it will set limits to what cultural (or other) groups can do to their members because it will have laws justified by the harm principle (and perhaps one or more of the principles discussed in chapter 4). That its laws are justified by the harm principle means that it will be warranted – and take itself to be warranted – in interfering in cases where a group harms one of its members. A group that wishes to sacrifice a member on the altar of some supposed god, for example, would rightly be interfered with when the sacrifice involves harming the member.

There is, of course, an important limitation to the aforementioned rightful interference – the action interfered with must actually be harmful, which means the person who is thought to be in a harmful situation (on the altar) did not consent to her position. Given *Volenti*, if she consents – genuinely, rationally, and with full information – there is no wrong and so no harm.

As should be obvious, such a group may be in an *unjust* society. If that is the case, the harm principle will still give us guidance as to when the group's activities can be interfered with, but there will be complications. Imagine, for example, that a group of Left Foot Worshippers (LFWs) is in a society wherein everyone is forced to have their left foot amputated at age 30, but an exception is made for religious opposition by LFWs. Others try to refuse having their feet amputated, but to no avail. The amputations are unjust but required by law, so the state is unjust. LFWs are, in this regard, lucky because the government exempts them (perhaps because they worshipped left feet long before the state was founded). But

Lefty Podriac, the High Priest of all LFWs, insists that all LFWs amputate the little toe on their right foot – and the LFW Guard enforces this dictate. If the society were just and an LFW wished to refuse this dictate, the state would protect her right to exit the group – she'd then able to keep her little right toe as well as her left foot. Since she would have this choice, if she chooses to stay in the LFW group, by *Volenti*, she cannot claim to be wronged when her little right toe is amputated – so she cannot claim to be harmed and no interference is permitted. In the unjust society that amputates left feet, though, the LFW – wishing not to have her little right toe amputated – is in a situation wherein she must choose between having that toe amputated and having her left foot amputated with no possibility of opting out of the situation. She is forced into the situation which is thus itself an injustice. In this case, it seems we can say that the amputation of her right toe is a harm – she has not consented to it (perhaps her society does not protect her right to exit; perhaps it does but then immediately amputates her left foot). Interference there – by anyone (international players included, as discussed below) – would be prima facie permissible. Let's continue, now, with the simplifying assumption that the domestic society is just.

Cultures are different in many ways. One of those concerns the second important factor mentioned above: membership. *Volenti* allows not merely that one might consent to a particular action sanctioned by one's group, but that conceivably one could give blanket consent to all such actions. Should one do so – should one be a member of the group in a fully voluntary way where that includes consenting to all of the group's rules and practices – then what happens within that group is not harm (in the sense relevant to the harm principle).

We should not kid ourselves. Most cultural groups are not as described in the previous paragraph: most people do not voluntarily join cultural groups at all, let alone in a way that can be plausibly taken to be consent to everything that occurs within its confines. Still, such groups can exist. A group that did not allow entrance into its ranks until the initiate was, say, 30 years old, could be as described above. Similarly, initiates could be required to take several critical thinking and philosophy classes before giving consent to full-fledged membership. It's difficult to imagine that someone in such a situation would join a group the rules of which would make it at all likely that one would be hurt, but it's not impossible. Still, the more typical situation is one wherein people are born into the group. Our discussion about that sort of situation is largely postponed until chapter 6B. Here, though, we can say that if a member of a group voluntarily exits her group or displays the intent to do so, there is clear indication that she does not consent to the group, and if the cultural group tries to assert its authority over her anyway, it likely runs afoul of the harm principle. There have been cases, for example, of tribal groups forcing alleged members to participate in tribal rites when the individuals in question denied their own membership (see *Thomas v. Norris*, a 1992 Canadian case; for discussion, see Eisenberg 1994; Dick 2011). Such acts count as harms and are not to be tolerated (according to the harm principle).

Nothing said here should be in any way surprising given what was said in chapter 3. Consistent with all that has been said throughout, if a group – cultural or otherwise – takes some action that has the effect of wrongfully setting back the interests of a *non-member*, the group causes a harm and interference is permissible. Similarly, if a group – cultural or otherwise – takes some action that has the effect of wrongfully setting back the interests of a *member*, the group causes a harm and interference is permissible. The action in either case, though, will simply not be wrongful if there is consent from the individual whose interests were set back.

Of course, groups may take actions that non-members – perhaps members of the broader society within which the group lives – may find distasteful or think immoral. If what has been said thus far is right, though, this will not be enough to warrant an end to toleration. Offensive actions by groups are no different, for our purposes, than offensive actions by individuals. In my view, harm and not offense is what justifies an end to toleration. Even a group that holds its "worship" meetings in weekly rides on buses, where all members ride the bus nude and participate in coprophagic sexual picnics, would have to be tolerated so long as there were no public health (harm) issues and all involved consented. Similarly, harmless immoral actions by groups are no different, for our purposes, from harmless immoral actions by individuals. Again, it is harm – and not mere immorality – that justifies interference in this view. Of course, as already admitted, you, Dear Reader, may consider the offense principle or legal moralism to be correct and have a way to defend one or both – in which case, you might think it right *not to tolerate* the sorts of activities just mentioned, whether from an individual or from a cultural group. Alternatively, you might have concerns raised by the presence of a cultural group that are not similarly raised by individuals acting alone – perhaps a thought that such groups have intrinsic value that must be balanced against the value of not allowing the activity. My view, though, is that cultural groups have no more intrinsic value than whole societies (as discussed in chapter 4D) – which is not to deny that harms can happen to individuals *as members of a group* (as discussed in chapter 4A).

What can be said about toleration internationally? Once again, our general framework serves us well. Only if there is harm – wrongful setback of interests – is there any moral warrant for interference. If no harm is present, there is no call for interference. Putting this in terms discussed in chapter 3E, the presence of harm makes interference permissible, but not necessarily required. The reasons that interference might be permissible but not required in the international arena are much the same as they are in the domestic arena, but include an additional factor.

In the domestic arena, we would not want to interfere with one-time Johnny, who intentionally and with much forethought flies to a city far away from his own, slaps some innocent bystander across the face, and then returns to the anonymity of his own home. He wrongfully sets back the interests (in not feeling pain, etc.) of that bystander, so interference is permitted. Nonetheless, the expenditures needed to interfere with Johnny likely far outweigh the benefits gained by interfering (to punish him, for example). So though we think interference is permitted, we do not push for it. This sort of situation occurs frequently in the international realm: the expenses that we would incur, for example, if we decided to intervene in the Chinese occupation of Tibet are enormous. It is fairly clear that the native Tibetans have had their interest in self-rule set back and, to my mind at least, fairly clear that the occupation is wrongful (I say this realizing it makes virtually certain this book will not be sold in China). If I am right, the Tibetans have been harmed – likely as individuals and also as members of a national group (again, as discussed in chapter 4A, individuals can be harmed *as members of a group*). Still, that this makes interference *permissible* does not end the investigation.

We should not pretend that the only costs with interference are monetary. There are significant moral costs involved in cases of international intervention. This is why standard just war theory, the historically most developed view on these matters, requires that there be a high probability of a successful outcome *without disproportional losses*. Sending armed (and even unarmed humanitarian) personnel to intervene in any situation on foreign territory – especially hostile enemy territory – can easily result in loss of life, not only of our own soldiers and those they fight, but also innocents on the ground, caught up in the crossfire or used as pawns (or shields) by either side. Given these potentially high non-monetary costs, even if international intervention is permissible, it may be incredibly unwise. Indeed, in an important sense, such an intervention may be *impermissible*. It may be permissible according to a too-simple application of the harm principle that does not consider all the likely results of the intervention. It may be *impermissible all things considered* even when there is harm present, because the costs that would result from the intervention are simply too great – including further harms!

One important reason that there are high costs to foreign interventions – even solely humanitarian intervention – is that states are considered *sovereign*. This is often thought of as analogous to the autonomy that sometimes serves as a guide to what can be done to persons. Just as it is wrong to interfere with a person (who has caused no harm) because it prevents her from acting on her autonomy (or "it infringes her autonomy"), many think it is wrong to interfere with a state because it prevents that state from acting on its sovereignty (or "it infringes her sovereignty").

Say we become aware of widespread female circumcision or female infanticide (or disenfranchisement of a minority or ...) in far-off ThirdLandia. Let's say that these are clearly harmful. The first sets back possible interests a female could have in enjoyable sexual relations and the second . . . – well, let's say the second sets back any possible interests she may have.[5] So, interference is permissible. But like many people in the world, ThirdLandians are patriotic and believe their country is their own and should remain sovereign, able to keep foreigners out. They are thus willing to fight to protect their land from "invaders" – even if they believe those invaders are there to help. The predictable result is that if we send humanitarian aid workers to help victims of female circumcision (or the amputation of left legs, to return to that example) and to seek to educate people so as to prevent that and the infanticide, they will have to fight. Some will be hurt. Even if such incidents would not be harms (which seems unlikely), being hurt is a bad thing and matters, morally, when determining what to do. (A cost can weigh against interference without being a harm; if this weren't the case, we would likely not only be warranted but also required to interfere whenever there was a harm, no matter how minor, unless there were a countervailing harm involved in the interference.)

Sovereignty and patriotism are important factors of the current world, for better or – and often – for worse. Some argue that there is moral value in sovereignty or in patriotism, but I am not taking that position. Indeed, if I had more space, I might argue against it. In any case, I will simply deny it here. But I cannot deny that patriotism matters in the world. People are willing to fight for their countries, arbitrary borders and all. Knowingly sending people – armed or not – to cross such borders is thus morally fraught. It may be the right thing to do in some cases, but not all. All the cases where it is the right thing to do will be cases where there is harm or a serious threat of harm. Not all cases where there is harm or a serious threat of harm will be cases where it is right to cross the border. Put differently, the (limited and derivative) importance of state sovereignty is a major concern, as are the practical effects of one state's interference in another state's affairs. If such interference will result in further harms, that counts against it – though perhaps not decisively. Indeed, there may be moral costs that weigh against interference without being harms. Clearly, there is much messiness here that needs more discussion than I can provide.[6]

Before moving on, we shall discuss one further international issue of much importance in our world. This is an issue that could just as easily be discussed at the end of the next subsection, as it involves international business. It also hearkens back to part of the discussion in chapter 4B: the idea that interference rather than toleration will be warranted in cases of systems with many people complicit in a harm that no one individual can be said to be responsible for.

Imagine a poor country with millions and millions of un- or under-employed individuals. Such a country would be an excellent source of labor for countries that have few unemployed. In some cases, people seeking work might emigrate to countries with more employment opportunities. In other cases, work sites (e.g., factories, processing facilities, call centers, etc.) might be set up in the poorer country so that businesses from richer countries could hire workers in their own land. This has a benefit for the workers in that they avoid relocation expenses and stay in their native land (which likely has a low cost of living). Of course, the benefit to the hiring firm is obvious: a large source of cheap labor. Now imagine that these work sites are in zones, legally specified by the host country as "export processing zones" (EPZs), wherein there are no legal protections for workers. Imagine further that the host country actually aids hiring corporations in a way meant to keep wages low within those zones. Imagine the host country even provides guards to prevent workers from leaving. In this sort of scenario, those of us who buy products in our countries produced in those EPZs are complicit in a system that results in the specified treatment of those employed there. Arguably those employed there are harmed – wrongfully forced to stay there against their will, for example (or forced to work in poor working conditions or . . .).

Now imagine a different scenario, though one that could fairly easily be combined with the one just outlined. Imagine a relatively poor country that discovers it sits on tremendous oil reserves. Though people there do not use extensive quantities of oil, the rulers of the country – both political and business leaders, who may be the same people – realize they can make a fortune selling the oil to American and European oil companies.[7] Some such leaders might use the revenue to better all the citizens of their country, of course. In other places, the rulers might decide to sell the oil and use the proceeds for their own benefit – including using them to pay for a stronger military to support their regime that, perhaps, is not well liked by many of its citizens. Perhaps they even use the proceeds to pay for military actions killing groups of people whom they see as a threat to their rule. In this sort of scenario, those of us who buy the oil from that country (and those of us who profit from companies selling them arms) are complicit in a system that results in the specified harms.

Finally, consider a relatively poor country with or without substantial resources to sell internationally. It is a feature of international society that governments can borrow money from international sources at lower rates than individuals can.[8] The reason for this is straightforward: the lender knows that the country will be there to repay the loan, no matter how long into the future. Well after a ruler borrows the money, his compatriots can pay it off. The current leader can impose debts on future generations. Even given a complete change in leadership – perhaps even a complete change in constitutional structure – the country will be obliged to repay the debt, since, if it does not, that country and its future leaders will face international censure and inability to borrow further. This strikes me as problematic enough, but it is worse than indicated thus far. Current leaders exercising their country's right to borrow money can use the money in any way they see fit – perhaps, again, using it to support a military that quashes any opposition, including, again, killing groups of people whom they see as a threat to their rule. In this sort of scenario, those of us who profit from banks that participate in loaning those leaders money (and those of us who profit from companies selling them arms) are complicit in a system that results in the specified harms.

In the above three sorts of cases (where we benefit from forcibly maintained EPZs, oil producers, or international loans that result in harms to individuals), those of us living in the developed world are complicit in a system that results in harm to citizens of relatively poor countries. If there were some entity capable of interfering with this system, the harm principle would clearly permit its interference – subject, of course, to the same sorts of worries discussed above with international military interventions. There is no such entity (that is willing) to interfere. What this means, I think, is simply that if anyone is to interfere, it is to be *us*. *We* can "interfere" ourselves and refuse to be complicit in the current systems that result in harms. We can alter our buying habits – and indeed our living habits – so as to not be complicit in these harms. Alternatively, we can participate in some activity or organization that seeks to redress the harms done. I can't here recommend precisely how this should occur, but interesting proposals have been made.[9]

We move on.

C　The business world

Throughout this book I have been making the case – implicitly – that normative principles of toleration, especially the harm principle, can be used to address many more concerns of political morality and justice than has usually been taken to be the case. It should no longer be surprising that such principles can also be used to determine when state actions in the economic arena are permissible – though I feel obliged to point out again that this way of discussing the economic arena is not currently standard.[10]

I suspect that most will quickly see that the harm principle is relevant when we are talking about whether or not the state can permissibly interfere with purchases that individuals make. Can the state permissibly make illegal – fail to tolerate – the sale, purchase, and use of marijuana by rational adults? Not if we take the strict version of the harm principle to be correct (as I do). Even if marijuana causes some medical damage (evidence suggests such damage is on a par with smoking tobacco), so long as the user is rational and knowledgeable, her use must be tolerated. Of course, it would be permissible to interfere with a sale of marijuana if the seller laces the marijuana with an undeclared substance without telling the buyer – for the buyer would not be in a position to buy it with informed choice. Similarly, of course, it is permissible to interfere with the sale to a minor, as minors are unlikely to be in a position to make a rational and informed choice.[11] Otherwise, though, the sale and purchase must be tolerated. The same would be true of other drugs. Of course, if it turns out that there is good evidence that the use of a particular drug is linked to increased harms *to others*, that would count as good reason, according to the harm principle, to interfere. Hence, if there is good evidence that cocaine or crack users have a statistically greater likelihood than non-users of causing harms to others (through battery, theft, or driving accidents, for example), the state can permissibly make such drugs illegal – or put limits on their use.[12] I take it this is what justifies laws against drinking and driving. Drunk drivers are significantly more likely to cause harm than sober drivers. It should be noted, though, that this sort of argument does not support an outright ban on the use of any drug. We need restrictions to prevent harm, but outright bans are an extreme sort of restriction. Another, less restrictive, requirement would be that the drugs can only be consumed in specified locations with mandatory supervision, paid for by the users who would be prevented from doing any harm. (It may also be that some harms related to drug use are partially the result of prices inflated by unwarranted government interventions and would be reduced or eliminated by the removal of such interventions.)

I should note that advocates of the offense principle, paternalism, or moralism, might argue that we would be right to interfere with the use of many drugs. They might find such activity offensive, they might think (correctly in many cases) that it damages the individuals using the drugs, they might think such use simply immoral (whether because damaging to society or not). As I argued in chapter 4, I do not find such arguments plausible, regardless of the subject. Importantly, though, *if you do*, you should consider whether such arguments would be plausible as applied to drugs.

Before moving away from issues involving the sale of illicit drugs, consider one way a society wedded to the harm principle as the sole principle of toleration would differ from our own. In our society, the following conversation between schoolchildren would raise eyebrows, but in my ideal society – where there are only laws that are properly justified by the strict version of the harm principle – it would not:

Alice: "My dad is a drug dealer."
Arty: "Well, my dad doesn't *help people* like yours, but he
          does entertain people – he's an actor."

Alice's statement would raise concerns in adults in our society because we tend to conceive of "drug dealers" as people that sell illegal drugs, often quite violent and short-lived. But in the ideal society where toleration reigns, drug dealers are simply purveyors of drugs, in the same line of work as any pharmacy today. They sell drugs – perhaps those that are not tolerated (or that are supposedly not tolerated) in our society and perhaps those that are. Perhaps some people in my ideal world would have negative views of drug dealers, but they would be in the same boat as those with negative views of actors (today and presumably in my ideal society). There will always be people that still have some opposition to others, whether based on the others' careers or something else. What matters is that in the ideal society, the state has a policy of toleration regarding such activities and individuals know that they too must not interfere with those others. This is, I think, a remarkable difference. In the ideal society, given that children could have such discussions, there is likely to be far less violence and theft associated with the sale of drugs.

The analysis offered above about drugs applies to "products" and services in the sex industry, where I take pornography and prostitution to be the main examples. In all cases, if the parties are rational and fully informed, they are free to participate in trades involving sex. In the sex trade, of course, it is extremely important that it is not only the buyer, but also the seller who must be rational and fully informed. Deceiving someone into providing sexual services (whether appearing in a picture or film or directly performing the service) is essentially defrauding that person, thus wronging them. If their interests are set back in the process (perhaps because they didn't want to be recorded or engage in the sexual activity), they are harmed and interference is warranted. Obviously, forcing someone to provide sexual services is a wrongful setback of their interest in controlling their life. Equally obviously, children are not capable of consenting to such activity, so even with their stated agreement (which does not count as fully rational) their participation is counted as wrongful and, the psychological evidence suggests, sets back their interests. Hence, it is obvious that interference – and not toleration – is warranted in all cases of child pornography and child prostitution. Unfortunately, although there are many laws against such activities, it remains widespread, with much child prostitution amounting to slavery.

Here again, I should note the possible role of other principles discussed in chapter 4. Clearly, many people find pornography and prostitution offensive. Clearly, many people think those purchasing these things (whether magazines, videos, or personal services) are hurting themselves. And clearly, many people think they are immoral. As indicated in chapter 4, though, I do not think these arguments will suffice to justify not tolerating the activity. Of course, I hope that people will agree that *child* pornography and prostitution are offensive and immoral – indeed that all non-voluntary pornography and prostitution are offensive and immoral – but this is not why I think we are right not to tolerate them. We are right not to tolerate them because they are harms. (It is not merely that they *cause* harms. They *are* harms. Forcing a child to engage in sexual activity, like beating her with a hammer, is doing harm to her.)

Let's step back from the heinous activities all agree (I believe and hope) we should not tolerate. There are other activities in the economic arena that are not heinous but are often reviled nonetheless and so worth discussing. In particular, the "outsourcing" of jobs and importing of goods. I turn to them.

As discussed in the previous subsection, countries with many unemployed citizens can attract employment opportunities by being friendly to multinational companies that open factories, call centers, and processing centers. Depending on how the policies involved are arranged, these may be perfectly moral and reasonable affairs, with workers treated well (though likely earning far lower wages than those working in the countries where the multinational corporations originate). That is, it may be that no one in the host country is harmed. Still, many in the US and Europe worry about using such labor because they fear losing jobs – they worry, that is, about the effect that outsourcing has on their own domestic unemployment rates. In contemporary politics, of course, this can be a hot button issue, with candidates for national office claiming that they will adopt policies to prevent the practice. Many in the US – not just politicians – often claim we should "buy American."

But why would we want to prevent the practice of outsourcing or the importation of goods made overseas? The popular idea is that when jobs migrate overseas to lower-paid laborers, it harms people domestically and so does not warrant toleration. If we adopt the strict version of the harm principle, as I have been recommending, though, this is almost certainly a mistake. A harm, we have said, is a wrongful setback to interests. The individuals who lose their jobs due to outsourcing might well have their interests set back, but it is hard to see how they are wronged in the process. Assuming their employer paid them for their past service and that they did not have a contract requiring further employment, it would seem that the employer is free to hire and fire whom she likes, no matter where the potential employee is. If that is right, she does no wrong when she fires (or "lets go" or "downsizes") employees domestically.

It should also be noted that while it's clear that some will have their interests set back, it is not clear that many would have *long-term* interests set back. Many will be able to find employment with a different business (or start their own), perhaps in a different industry. Some may need additional education or training before doing so, but they may then end up working in a more satisfying position (I assume more schooling or training leads to more satisfaction). Admittedly, some – primarily older workers – will be far worse off, unable to ever find a new work situation. Those people may well need help. For the rest, though, there is clear hope for new and better employment.

There is further reason, though, to think that outsourcing on balance contributes to forwarding people's interests, not setting them back. Quite simply, when labor is outsourced, it migrates to areas where wages are lower. Lower wages mean lower costs for the production of goods. Lower costs for the production of goods means lower prices for purchasers of those goods. Lower prices for those goods means consumers have greater ability to do more with their resources (income and savings). A clear benefit to many.

The argument of the previous paragraph may sound surprising (at least to those who have not studied economics), but should not. Consider that the prices of televisions and computers have consistently fallen and when the price stays the same, what is purchased does considerably more than what would have been bought five years before. The iPad I am now writing on, for example, cost $500 and does about as much as the $1500 computer I purchased 12 years ago. That computer, in turn, did far more than the computer I purchased for roughly the same amount 10 years before that. Consider, for another example, the ubiquitous iPhone – an item that can be purchased (without a contract) for about $500. For that price, you get a phone you can take anywhere, an alarm clock/watch, a radio, a calculator, a portable way to carry music – and photography and video – collections, a still camera, a video camera, a GPS device, an e-reader, a remote control, a gaming device, and more. Many of these items would have been unthinkable 50 years ago. You could have them all 10 years ago, but at much greater cost and inconvenience. It may be that the iPhone could be made domestically, but it's unclear what advantage that would provide.

No one should have the impression that this discussion is only about electronic goods. I have a neighbor, in her sixties, who tells me she did not like spinach when she was younger but came to realize that this was because the only spinach her mother could buy was canned spinach. I don't think I have ever even *seen* canned spinach. Today, we can buy fresh spinach no matter when, grown in parts of the world suitable to its cultivation at that time of year and shipped to our local markets. As far as I can tell, we should be grateful for this.[13] I am not a big fan of spinach, but the case parallels that of other fruits, vegetables, and flowers. Indeed, it is one of the benefits to international trade – which is what outsourcing amounts to – that if one lives in a drought-ridden area, one can import food. Those who oppose importing food (and electronics and anything else), then, should surely tolerate it since, given the above arguments, no one is harmed and so much is gained.

In short, when we hear people arguing against out-sourcing, we should evaluate the effects on everyone – not just the vocal and obvious few who are hurt. This is especially true when those hurt will be able to recover, but it is true even when some will not – for that their interests are set back does not mean they are harmed. And, again, many benefit.[14]

The pattern of argument should now be clear: in the business realm, an item should only be illegal (that is, not tolerated) if its production or sale involves a harm. That sort of analysis is relevant to a great many questions individuals have about business, but in today's world, it is not enough. The rise of the corporate model of business was a game-changer – especially when those corporate entities are, as they are in the US, considered legal persons. The corporate model of business facilitates interactions between many people, allowing easier pooling of resources so as to allow economies of scale. It does this, in part, by protecting the corporation against failures by the corporation's owners and by protecting the corporation's owners against failures by the corporation. Since all are protected, they are more willing to pool resources. But more on that in a moment.

Persons are rational beings who form intentions. Many are autonomous in that they form intentions and beliefs that are independent of the intentions and beliefs of others and that are revisable upon reflection. Corporate entities are not like that. Corporate entities are simply groups of individuals, organized according to specified rules and regulations. Indeed, I would suggest that corporate business entities are morally on a par with cultural groups – which are also groups of individuals, organized according to specified rules and regulations. Admittedly, the rules and regulations of cultural groups are often inchoate rather than explicit. This matters for many reasons. The fact that people abide by implicit rules in a cultural group may, for example, be a distinguishing characteristic, allowing them to identify one another in a way that members of the corporate group that is IBM may not be able to. Nonetheless, none of that speaks to harms or consent, so none of that should matter for determining when toleration may permissibly end.

When I spoke of cultural groups in the last section, I indicated that if people consent to be hurt by their group, toleration is called for. If businesses are on par with cultural groups, then the same would be true when talking about business groups – i.e., corporations (or partnerships, etc.). Adult voluntary employees of a corporation cannot claim to be harmed (in the sense relevant to the harm principle) when the corporation acts on rules the employees knew of when they agreed to work there. Of course, a change in those rules makes it possible that the harm principle is violated. But if the corporate policy was clearly "one factor involved in evaluation for promotion or salary increase is the willingness to perform sexual favors for one's supervisor," and an employee agrees, it is hard to see how she can complain that she is wronged when passed over for a promotion because she would not perform the favor. Similarly, if the policy was clearly "we will be pumping a gaseous form of chemical X into the workplace because we have evidence that it increases productivity; please be aware that there is also evidence that it increases the probability that you will get cancer," and an employee agrees, it is hard to see how she can complain. Of course, in both cases, corporations making such declarations are likely to face difficulty in hiring employees. Rational people are likely to seek employment in friendlier environments.[15] This may be the most important reason corporations seek to make their work environments hospitable – if they do not, rational people would only work there if they had no better options or there was a significant (likely monetary) premium on their compensation. In all likelihood, the most talented people will work elsewhere.

Of course, as with cultural groups and purveyors of currently illicit contraband, the acts of a corporation can have effects on people who do not voluntarily participate with them. They do this, for example, when they pollute (as discussed in section A of this chapter). Such cases are easily shown to involve real harms that warrant a decisive end to toleration. Similar arguments apply to recent cases involving corporations like Enron, AIG, and British Petroleum. In each case, people who were not consenting participants were hurt – and in a way that seems prima facie wrongful. The British Petroleum case seems clear: oil in the water on one's shorefront property or where one fishes is clearly a setback to one's interests. If proper precautions to prevent such spills were not taken, it also seems likely to be wrongful. Thus there seem to be obvious harms – and so a permissible end to toleration.

The scandals of the other companies may be more difficult to assess, but not that difficult. Assuming Enron officials intentionally manipulated the price of energy in its favor by taking wrongful actions, it wrongfully set back the interests of those whose energy prices were affected (their interest in paying less). Perhaps AIG's case is the hardest to analyze. Putting simply what happened here (that we are concerned with) is that AIG sold insurance for financial derivatives called collateralized debt obligations (or CDOs) – basically, packages of loans that theoretically included loans from people with a high likelihood of repaying the debt as well as loans from people highly *unlikely* to repay the debt. But it was more complicated than that. The CDOs were packages of packages – and in some cases, insurance on such packages. I cannot here delve further into the details. The important point, in fact, is that very few people understood what was being bought and sold – i.e., what those packages were. This is important because, in order to provide insurance for something, one must be able to understand it. Life insurance companies (*all* insurance companies) hire actuaries to determine how much they must charge in order to make a profit by estimating likely payouts. If the item insured is such that actuaries cannot do a reasonable job determining likely payouts, the insurance company cannot responsibly sell the insurance. In selling such insurance, AIG violated its fiduciary responsibility to its stockholders. That is, it wrongfully set back their interests. It harmed them. Toleration rightly can end. (More simply: the practice can be prohibited.) Given how extensive its holdings were, AIG also ended up wreaking havoc on much of the economy – because many large institutions relied on that insurance. It is not hard to see that this caused harms.

It is important, in discussing the sort of issues raised in this section, to say something about what sort of real change would be mandated if we were to take seriously the view that the strict version of the harm principle is the correct normative principle of toleration. The harm principle is an interesting principle in that it tells us (a) interference is permitted when there is harm, but not (b) what to do when interfering and not (c) what specific actions are harms. Given the analysis of harm provided in chapter 3C, it is clear that context matters. Bernie Madoff's actions apparently cost a lot of people a lot of money. Some of those people seem to have known more about Madoff's scheme than others. Those with full knowledge of the scheme when they got involved may have had their interests set back, but not wrongfully. They were thus not harmed and their setback is no cause for interference. Of the rest, some may have had more knowledge than others, and thus be less wronged. The setbacks in all the cases may be the same (or vary only in amount of money lost), but the wrong varies. That means the harm varies, and, presumably, the sort of interference permitted varies. (What sort of punishments can be meted out varies, but so too do the sorts of regulations that can be put in place to prevent future acts like Madoff's.)

Importantly, the harm principle can be used at a higher level of policy than suggested thus far. We might want to use it as a basic principle of justice, to use Rawls's terms, such that a society is considered just only if the basic structure of that society is designed to minimize harm. Putting this point differently: we can invoke the harm principle to justify interference when a harm is or would be committed, and we can invoke the harm principle to determine how we should set things up in the first place. Most of the book has been about the first of these. Here, it's worth considering the latter: what sorts of rules should be in place to prevent harm from happening?

Here is a quick guess: given *Volenti*, all fully voluntary trades must be tolerated. Of course, less than fully voluntary trades might not be tolerated. Given that, the social-economic system should encourage business entities to be sure that all trades are voluntary. Truth-in-advertising laws are clearly one part of this. Another is a simple corollary of that: all questions asked by potential trading partners (customers, buyers, sellers, what-have-you) must be answered truthfully. Any proof that advertising includes lies or that questions are answered dishonestly – that is, any attempt to be less than fully upfront with trading partners – would suggest a wrong. Given a setback of interests, there would be a harm and thus a permissible end to toleration.

If we were to take this seriously, we might seek to better educate consumers (everyone) about how to ask good probing questions. Consider, for example, the claim by a cellular phone company to provide "unlimited internet access." It's worth asking that company what this means. Does it include unlimited email, both received and sent? Unlimited use of graphically interfaced access to everything on the internet – or merely text-based? Perhaps most relevant today, does it leave it possible that the cell phone company will provide that access at varying (decreasing) speeds when your usage increases? For a second sort of example, consider the simple and oft-used claim that "no one beats our prices."[16] Here it's worth asking not only if others match the prices, but also if others sell exactly the same goods, with the same names and product numbers. Many products – beds, for example – can be produced with multiple names and model numbers to help stores make positive-sounding but useless claims. Here's an example of what I have in mind. Producer A manufacturers 100,000 units of a particular type of bed. All 100,000 units are the same. Producer A then labels 20,000 of those units "Model 12001, Super-Comfy-Sleep," another 30,000 "Model 1201, Super Sleeper," and the remaining 50,000 "Model 121, Comfort Sleep." Those labeled "Model 12001" are sold to a high-end store that sells each unit for $1000, those labeled "Model 1201" are sold to a mid-range store that sells each unit for $750, and those labeled "Model 121" are sold to a large discount retailer that sells each unit for $500. When the high-end store advertises Model 12001 at $1000, it proudly claims that no one beats its prices. Strictly speaking, this is true. No one else even sells Model 12001, so no one else can beat the price. But this is also deceptive, since the same model bed – with a different model number and name – can be bought for much less. Since the high-end retailer does not lie in its advertising, it is only by asking further questions that one can know if one is getting a good deal. Of course, in our world, the high-end retailer would likely have hired salespeople who either do not know about this arrangement or who were prepared to avoid the question. That, I am suggesting, is what should not be permitted. Questions must be answered honestly.[17]

I will briefly suggest one further possibility regarding the sort of rules that should be in place if we take the harm principle seriously as a basic principle of justice. I said above that I thought corporations and cultural groups were morally on a par. They are not, though, *legally* on a par – because the corporate model is a legal framework. At root, this means corporations receive legal assistance at their inception. Cultural groups *might* receive assistance *as groups* – if, for example, the government gives tax breaks to the group – but such assistance can come only *after* the group exists, and contingently at that. By contrast, it is intrinsic to the corporation to receive assistance from the legal system. As a corporation, a business entity enjoys benefits not had by non-incorporated rivals – chiefly, limited liability, entity shielding, and asset lock-in (see Ciepley 2013 and Hansmann et al. 2006). Limited liability relieves individual investors of liability for the debts of the corporation, entity shielding protects the corporation from liability for the debts of its investors, and asset lock-in prohibits an investor (i.e., partial owner) from taking assets of the corporation. These protect the corporation in a way that single-proprietor businesses and partnerships are not protected – and, of course, in a way that cultural groups are not protected. Consider limited liability rules. If I am injured by the activity of a corporation (perhaps hit by a corporate-owned truck or made sick by corporate-produced pollution) and the corporation's assets are not sufficient to compensate me for the injury, I would remain uncompensated even though the corporation's owners (even if there is only one) have extensive wealth (see Hansmann and Kraakma 1991). This means that the corporate form itself allows harms to go unrectified. But there is a further element. According to the strict version of the harm principle, interference is only permitted if there is harm. Hence, the interference that allows for the corporate form – the legal framework instantiated by the government – is itself not permitted by the harm principle. My suggestion, then, is that a full commitment to the harm principle as the sole principle of toleration would leave us having to do away with the corporate form as it currently exists – with all its built-in legal protections. (Admittedly, there are likely ways for individuals to reconstruct the benefits of the corporate form through contract law. Admittedly, also, businesses can currently be incorporated under different rules; the three discussed above, though, are common.) This would leave business entities legally on a par with cultural groups, as I think is fitting.

6
Children and the Paradoxes of Toleration and Liberalism

As should be clear, normative principles of toleration provide us a powerful tool. We can discuss when individuals are required to tolerate other individuals and when they should be tolerated as well as when powerful groups – cultures, churches, businesses and others – should tolerate and when they should be tolerated and when states themselves should tolerate and when they should be tolerated. Despite the advantages, discussion of toleration inevitably leads to some theoretical difficulties.

A   The paradox of toleration

Many worry about the paradox of toleration: that we might be required to tolerate P, who does not tolerate X, which we think should be tolerated. (Alternatively: that our commitment to toleration will have us *not* tolerating intolerance.) That is, morally, we might have to engage in toleration of morally wrong acts of non-toleration. For example, we might think ourselves bound to tolerate a devil-worshipping group that physically punishes any of its members who enter a Catholic Church. Entering such a building transgresses no defensible normative principle of toleration. For a different example, we might think we should tolerate an Amish community that banishes one of its members, leaving him no means of survival, after he violates one of their religious rules that we do not accept. We often think toleration is called for in such cases so that different religions can survive and their members can live according to their own conception of the good life. But then we find ourselves tolerating actions that fail to tolerate things we think it wrong not to tolerate.

Perhaps there are genuinely paradoxical cases of toleration, but there are not many. There is no paradox in the first case above, for example. Worries there arise only when the member of the devil-worshipping group is thought to be under the control of the group against her will. The paradox disappears if she is a member of the group by her own choice. If she consents to the group, she consents to its rules, including the rule that would have her punished for entering a church. Tolerating the behavior of the group, then, is on a par with tolerating the winning boxer in a match: both boxers consent, so *Volenti* implies there is no wrong done to the losing boxer (who is hurt) and hence no reason for interference. The same can be said about the Amish case. We tolerate intolerance when all affected consent. If this is a paradox, it is easily explained (by *Volenti*).

Of course, as noted in the second section of the last chapter (5B), individuals are often members of religious groups without having consented to such membership. Many are born with a religious affiliation and accept that religion and its church hierarchy without thought. Especially when they are young, they cannot be thought of as consenting to the group's rules. In response to this fact, some suggest parents can consent on behalf of their children, as if by proxy. It's not clear why we should accept this. After all, in the typical proxy case, one adult consents to another adult casting a vote for her and this is not what happens with children – for if they can't consent to the group because of their age, they can't, because of their age, consent to nominate their parents as proxy.

It is sometimes claimed that the child's consent is not necessary (which is a good thing since they are not yet capable of giving it) for the parents to hold proxy. We are told that parents can act as proxies for their children because they act in the best interests of their children. But it's not clear what the best interests of children are (see Archard 2003) and it's not clear that all parents do act with their children's interests in mind. In the sorts of cases that would arise here – cases where a child has its interests set back by the community – the idea that parents hold proxy for their children is especially problematic. If we assume that parents have a valid proxy for their children, we essentially give up the hope of helping children. If the parent claims it is in the best interest of the child to be sacrificed so as to improve the prosperity of the group, for example, we would be unable to interfere – if we take the proxy as consent, *Volenti* means the child is not harmed. If the culture requires female circumcision and the parents use their proxy consent, there is no harm. Without arguing that there are harms in these sorts of cases, it is surely *not clear that there aren't*. Similarly, if the parent claims the child does *not* consent to the activity that results in its interests being set back, we simply have to conclude that the child *is* harmed, no matter the facts of the case. This is obviously not right.

What we should conclude from this discussion, then, is neither that there is harm present nor that there is not, but that parents cannot claim a unilateral proxy for their children and that, as such, consent cannot mitigate all setbacks to children's interest.[1] *Volenti*, then, is simply not relevant when discussing the sorts of cases where children cannot themselves consent. Thinking it is because parents act as proxy for their children makes it too easy for the parents and their cultures.

What this means for the paradox is simple. If there is consent, *Volenti* dissolves the paradox. If there is not consent – as when we are talking of children incapable of giving consent themselves – *Volenti* does not dissolve the paradox, but the paradox does not arise at all. Given lack of consent (admittedly difficult to discern in many cases), if the individual is harmed, interference is warranted as the group violates the harm principle. This is true, of course, even of adults if they have not consented. In short, in most cases, either *Volenti* dissolves the paradox by removing the harm and ruling out interference, or there is harm and interference is permitted.

B Children

I've noted, both in the last section and in chapter 5B, that we (usually) enter cultural groups upon birth – without our consent, but not against our wishes – and that this matters for determining if we are harmed by activities of such groups. The same is, in fact, true of our positions in our families. We don't consent to be raised by our parents any more than we consent to be born in our country of origin. Of course, in neither case do we seek to withhold consent. We simply are not the sorts of beings, as young children, who can consent. This means, very clearly, that *Volenti* does not apply to children. Just as we would not – and could not – ask a dog if he consents to a haircut, we would not – and could not – ask newborns if they consent to live with their parents. Whether those parents are good at parenting or not is a matter of luck as far as the newborns are concerned.[2] So too, of course, whether or not they are in a good culture is a matter of luck as far as they are concerned.

Some may find that last claim – and perhaps the one immediately before it – unacceptable, thinking we cannot judge cultures, and perhaps parents, as better or worse. This is a common and interesting claim, but almost certainly false. If the arguments of chapter 3C are correct, there is good reason to think there are objective claims in morality. Why cultures should be exempt from this, I do not know. In any case, it seems quite clear that a culture that encourages indiscriminate killing, stealing, and the like is not as good as a culture that encourages peace and well-being. Indeed, the former sort of culture could not continue to exist for long (see Rachels 1999: ch. 2). There is very good reason for the fact that all existing cultures have rules against these activities! Much more needs to be said about this, of course, but here I am willing to say that Nazi culture is not as good, for example, as Tibetan culture. I take this to be uncontroversial. There will, of course, be other cultures that, while very different from one another, cannot (at least not easily) be judged better or worse than each other because by any salient characteristic they are too similar morally to make such a call. There will be cultures – perhaps many cultures – that, while very different from each other, are morally on a par with one another. All this can also be said about parents as well. Parents who routinely abuse their children, leave them in a closet all the time, throw boiling water on them, starve them, or rape them are simply not good parents. Other parents might be better or worse than one another (at parenting); in some cases they will be equally good and, in some cases, we will not be able to (easily) judge which are better and which worse. From the infant's perspective, though, to what parents and into which culture she is born is mere luck – for better or worse.

Moral and political philosophers disagree about what to do with luck. Consider a simple case. Jack and Jill both leave a bar drunk and get in their cars and drive home. They drive parallel paths, as their homes are one street apart, equidistant from the bar. Jack gets home safely with no problem. No one was on the street he traveled. Jill was not so lucky. An infant managed to leave its home and crawl into the street where Jill was driving. She didn't see it until it was too late (her reflexes would have been better had she not been drinking). Jill is arrested for driving while intoxicated. Here's the thing: Jack did exactly the same thing(s) that Jill did and only because of luck made it home safe without hitting anyone. Why should Jill be punished when Jack is not? The disagreement here is simple: some think Jack should be punished in the same way as Jill since they did all the same things, while others think only Jill should be punished – the latter think luck can be a deciding factor when considering punishment (and other issues). In political philosophy, there is a bit more consensus that luck does not – or, rather, should not – matter. At least it should not matter for the outcome of lives.

Put the point this way: perhaps you were born to a relatively wealthy (perhaps middle-class) family that valued education and taught you to work hard. They were able to feed and clothe you well. By contrast, Bob was born to a poor family living in a bad area of town. Bob's parents frequently fed him overly processed foods because they were the least expensive. Bob's parents also worked long hours and so could not read to him or explain to him why he should work hard. Bob was left to fend for himself in a noisy apartment where he found it hard to sleep. Is it surprising in such a situation that Bob did not fare as well as you? The luck of the (birth) draw matters. Absent the sorts of foods that provide nutrients to the body and brain, one is less likely to perform well in school. Absent a quiet place to sleep (and study), one is less likely to perform well in school. Absent role models that not only claim school is important but model that belief, one is less likely to perform well in school. Absent people to help with homework and studying, one is less likely to perform well in school. That Bob was missing these things was, again, a matter of luck as far as he was concerned – he could not have done anything to bring them about.

The obvious question, at this point is, simply: "Should luck be tolerated?" That is meant as a joke – but only partly. Many political philosophers write as if luck should not be tolerated. They insist that anything that is due to luck is fair game for political intervention. If you think I am joking about *that*, do some research on "luck egalitarianism." I may be mocking that view, but I don't mean to mock it entirely. There is a clear place for not tolerating bad luck – the case we are discussing here: children.

Children, as we saw above, do not deserve their lot. Bob did not deserve to be born to his parents and Steve Jobs's and Bill Gates's children did not deserve to be born to their parents. They didn't deserve the superb living conditions, food, and education that their parents could buy them any more than Bob deserved the poorer conditions his parents provided for him. Nor did any of these individuals – or anyone else – deserve the love their parents showered them with or failed to shower them with. None of this says anything about Bob or the Jobs's or Gates's children as people – they may deserve great things (or not) as the adults they grow into. The point is that newborn children do not deserve the situations they are born into, because they did not do anything to deserve it. This is especially problematic, I think, when we are talking of children born into poverty – much too large a number. They don't deserve to be born into a situation where they cannot have adequate nutrition, healthcare, etc. If I choose to live in a rat-infested home without clean water, that is a choice I could (but would not) make. Should I make such a choice, I cannot claim to be harmed by my landlord. I consented and *Volenti* makes this hurt (I assume it's that) something other than a harm. But children born into such conditions (or worse) did not consent to – and do not deserve – their condition.[3] Children born to well-off but abusive parents did not consent to their abuse. The former – those born into poverty – may not be harmed by anyone in particular; if we assume their parents are doing the best they can, we assume their parents do not wrong them. The latter – those who are abused – are harmed (I assume that what we call abuse is wrongful and a setback to the child's interests).

It is an unfortunate fact of modern life – and perhaps has always been the case – that many children suffer. Suffering is bad. We can render this into terminology we have been using throughout: many children have their interests set back and when the children are very young, this happens, of necessity, without their consent. In many cases, it happens wrongfully.

Thus, a difficult question: what is the normative principle that determines when interference with treatment of children is and is not permitted? If it is the harm principle, it needs to be understood that *Volenti* cannot be invoked – wrongfulness cannot be commuted into something acceptable by any claim that a child consented, as we saw in the previous section. The problem, though, is more complicated. Someone who maliciously beats a child, harms the child. An abusive (physically or emotionally) parent harms their child – wrongly setting back the child's interests. What should we say, though, about the parent who does the best she can to promote *what she considers* the child's interests which she believes includes shunning medical care (consider the relatively benign refusal, by Jehovah's Witnesses, to accept blood transfusions), rejecting education (consider *Wisconsin v. Yoder*), or feeding the child only hot dogs, soda, and other similarly nutrition-lacking foods (all too common)? Such would likely set back the long-term interests of the child, though whether it was wrongful is unclear and *the child may have no idea she has or will have such interests.*

Determining the interests of a child is difficult work. Some believe that only real, currently existing, interests *ever* matter in determinations of harm; others think even adults have *ideal interests* they may not recognize (and that these can be wrongly set back). In previous chapters, I assumed it is real interests that matter for determinations of harm. When dealing with children, though, I will assume that ideal interests have to be considered for the simple reason that children are not yet capable of understanding much that is in their interest. A child might desire to eat ice cream for all meals and snacks and this may well be an interest, but the child also has an interest – whether he knows it or not – in ingesting adequate nutrition. The latter interest contradicts the first and should, it seems to me, take priority – though the child may not think so.

Notice that the (ideal) interest in adequate nutrition is shared by all biological beings, including newborn infants, who may have only one real interest – an interest we can assume any sentient being has: an interest in not suffering. (That there is such an interest seems clear when we recognize that when it suffers, a being recoils, trying to avoid the suffering.) We can't talk of any other real interests an infant would have. We cannot say that an infant has a real interest in nutrition or in learning math, physics, history, or anything else – for an infant does not even have those concepts so cannot possibly form the thought "I want to learn philosophy." It's nonetheless clear that talk of the interests of children, including infants, beyond that of not suffering is sensible. It makes sense to think of a child as having an interest in getting the sort of education that makes it possible for it to flourish in its society. Indeed, it makes sense to think all children have an interest in flourishing – though they do nothing to indicate any pursuit of a good life and though they don't formulate the thoughts. So, I will assume we can reasonably talk of ideal interests of children.

Despite the plausibility of the idea, it is not at all clear what ideal interests a child would have. Surely she has an interest in a satisfying life, but what that entails is unclear – more than basic nutrition to be sure, but what of a college education, piano lessons, or expensive clothing? This issue is owed far more extensive attention than I can provide here (see Archard 2003: 38–52 for some discussion). Indeed, the entire question of how to deal with children – for us, that means "What should be tolerated in the way children are raised, treated, educated, etc.?" – is in need of far greater attention than it has thus far received. For our purposes, it is important to note that to the extent that we cannot determine the interests of a child, we cannot determine when harm is done her – and so to that extent the harm principle is not sufficient as a normative principle of toleration (since it would not help us determine when toleration is required in these cases). If that were the case, another principle would be needed – a separate principle of parental responsibility that indicates what sorts of obligations adults have to children (or child-like adults), whether or not the failure to satisfy those obligations results in harm. Failure to live up to those obligations would be reason for interference. Stating that as a principle: "*Failure to satisfy the obligations one has to children (or child-like adults), whether or not the failure to satisfy those obligations results in harm, is warrant for interference.*"

This principle of parental responsibility may sound plausible. It may sound like an advance on the harm principle when discussing children. Some may think we should accept it as a second normative principle of toleration (or a third or fourth if one accepts any of the other principles discussed in chapter 4). This may be the case, but only if further work is done to explain what the obligations are that one has to children. I suspect that such work would bring us full circle – we have obligations to keep children from harm. Given that suspicion – which I cannot verify here – my own view is that we must seek to determine the interests of a child on a case-by-case basis and continue to use the harm principle alone. We must recognize that determining the interests of a child is difficult work with little in the way of additional principles to guide us. Nonetheless, it is not as though we are completely out to sea. We know children have an interest in not being abused, in being provided a home, shelter, clothing, adequate nutrition, love, playtime, etc.[4] And parents can often understand other interests their children have as they arise. My son, for example, clearly has an interest in playing with toy trains, watching videos of real and animated trains, and riding on trains. While he may not decide, later in life, to become a train conductor, I would surely be in the wrong if I set back his interest in trains by throwing away all his train things for no reason – or because, although he might have a good life as a conductor, I somehow thought this was not an acceptable life for him. This would be a harm.

With sufficient sensitivity, I think, we can use the harm principle in many if not all cases when we are concerned to determine what should be tolerated with regard to adult actions toward children. Indeed, despite the many flaws that exist in current legal systems, we actually do work with (something like) the harm principle when it comes to children. State departments of family and child services and child protective service agencies all interfere with the raising of children when some form of harm (whether intentional or neglectful) is reported. Once a child is in the system, the social workers involved work for reunification with the birth family where that is feasible. They might require the parent(s) to take parenting classes, prove they have "cleaned up" (for example, by going through a rehabilitation program for addicts), and accept mandatory supervision for some period of time, but they generally seek reunification. Should that not be possible, they seek to place the child elsewhere, in a safe – that is, harm-free – environment. We could also say that they will seek to place the child with people who can and will satisfy their incurred obligations to the child. While that is compatible with use of the principle of parental responsibility mentioned above, it does not provide that principle any advantage over the harm principle. Social workers investigate reported instances of neglect and abuse and provide analyses of harm done. Using such analyses with the harm principle seems likely to be useful.

A final comment about this sort of work. It is likely worth noting that even when the interests of a child are well defined, care is needed to balance the interests of the child against those of her parents or cultural or religious group. If we assume all children have a right to needed medical care, for example, and insist that certain procedures occur despite the protest of parents, we risk unduly failing to tolerate the parents and their religion. This is analogous to our analysis of international toleration: we may determine that interference rather than toleration is permissible when we look only at part of the issue, but we need to look at the full set of circumstances to determine if we should in fact interfere. Just as attacking China to free Tibet might be morally wrong even though the Chinese government violated the harm principle (as such an attack would result in the deaths of thousands and destabilize the world), there may be cases where interfering with how a family raises a child is too risky (morally speaking), even if it is known that they are harming the child. I would expect (and hope) that there would be few cases like this that involved serious harm to the child. Much will depend on the nature of the harm to the child, of course. My wrongly setting back my son's interest in watching train videos, for example, is unlikely to weigh heavily enough to interfere even though it is a harm (though some might try to rationally persuade me to let him watch them). The harm done him and my wife and me by interference is likely weightier. Malevolent Melody's burning her daughter, by contrast, is certainly likely to warrant interference even with all other harms (etc.) taken into consideration. What of the parent that feeds her child only hot dogs and soda and similarly nutrition-lacking food? Such cases will be less clear, but this is not enough to conclude that the harm principle is mistaken or insufficient. There may be no better principle available. And moral questions are often quite difficult to answer definitively (which does not mean there is no objective answer).

C The paradox of liberalism (and no autonomism)

Perhaps, then, no further principle is necessary for dealing with children. As discussed, the harm principle seems capable of providing principled responses for dealing with cultural groups (and other issues with children). As briefly discussed in section A, the supposed paradox of toleration does not seem very problematic. So perhaps we are done. That is, perhaps we are at a point where we can say: "Yes, we can now defend adequate normative principles of toleration that tell us when we must tolerate and when we might interfere. Nothing further is needed, except perhaps showing why toleration in general is important." But some offer a further worry: can the state interfere with those seeking an end to the regime of toleration? Or must the state tolerate those who seek to end the regime of toleration? This is the supposed "paradox of liberalism" – that liberalism as a commitment to extensive toleration cannot tolerate those who seek to end toleration. Given that toleration (or the value undergirding it) is objectively valuable, if this is a paradox, it's not worrisome. Those committed to the strict harm principle as the correct principle of normative toleration will simply respond that interference is not permitted against non-harmful (e.g., speech) acts, but is permitted against such actions that are harmful. This is the limit to toleration specified in the harm principle.

What if the harm principle itself should be rejected? More modestly, what if others in our society reject it? Can liberals force compliance with the principle and still claim to favor toleration? Would it not be endorsing a particular conception of the good life that some might reject? Some liberal theorists do insist on promoting autonomy (Mill sometimes seems to, but overall does not; Kant does), but endorsing the harm principle does not require it. As discussed above in section A, the advocate of toleration can admit that some groups limit their members' liberty (or autonomy) and allow that such must be tolerated – provided no one in that group is forced into it and no one in the group harms anyone outside the group. While we should admit that this provision can (and likely will) burden some groups, we should also recognize that such a burden would be the result of fair and equal treatment, not unfair. After all, kosher meat is more expensive than non-kosher meat and the differential burden that Jews and Muslims face given this price disparity is not unfair (see Barry 2001: 24–40, 118–31). We don't say, in that case, that there is anything that is to be done to alleviate the differential burden. Similarly, there seems little reason to think there is anything that is to be done to alleviate the differential burden caused some groups by a commitment to the harm principle as the sole principle of normative toleration. Groups that seek to impose their will on others, prohibiting those others from engaging in non-harmful activity of any sort (sexual, intoxication-inducing, etc.), are simply out of luck if the harm principle is the sole principle of toleration.[5] More clearly, they are out of luck unless they can offer a defense of moralism or some other normative principle of toleration that would require that people not engage in the activities they seek to ban. Absent the defense of such a principle, they are not allowed to use force – their own or that of the state – to interfere with others unless those others are causing harm.

To be clear,[6] the requirement that force not be used on individuals against their will is not a requirement to promote autonomy. The concern is only with harm. Individuals can certainly be harmed by having their autonomy wrongly set back, but they can also be harmed by having their interest in conforming to a group – that is, an interest in being non-autonomous – wrongly set back. Some reasonably prefer to have their autonomy curtailed and nothing in the harm principle suggests this is impossible or something permitting interference. We can think no one has the right to coerce others against their will without assuming all individuals have an interest in being autonomous. In this way, freedom from harm is interestingly more basic than autonomy: even those who wish to have their autonomy curtailed should be tolerated. Perhaps Cindy wishes to accept a subordinate role to her husband. We may (rightly) believe that Cindy would be better off in a more egalitarian marriage, but if we try to persuade her of this claim (as discussed in chapter 3E, rational persuasion is not interference), and she decides she'd rather have the life of a subordinate wife, we cannot interfere. Doing otherwise might promote Cindy's autonomy but would do so by forcing her to act against her interests. Putting the point differently: both the individual who has her autonomy infringed against her will and the individual who has her autonomy *promoted* against her will are forced to act against their interests. Both have their interests set back and, plausibly, wrongly, so bring the harm principle to bear, indicating a warranted end to toleration. (Notice that not all harms are bodily; some are infringements of *the freedom of conscience* – whether an infringement of autonomy or coerced autonomy. Indeed, I suspect all harms involve an infringement of the freedom of conscience, though many also include bodily harm. If you punch me in the face, you prevent me living in accord with my conscience and you wrongfully cause me pain.)

Nothing I have said thus far leads to the conclusion that the paradox of liberalism is less than a paradox, but paradoxes are not contradictions; they can be lived with. Liberals can live with the paradox of liberalism because of the objective value of toleration. (They need not insist everyone recognize that objective value.) Unsurprisingly, all liberal theorists agree that we need not tolerate actions intended to bring about the end of the regime of toleration that is the liberal state. They all agree that toleration is of value but recognize that a regime of toleration has limits such that it will not tolerate the end of toleration. Similarly, a Christian regime would not tolerate the end of Christianity and a Jewish regime would not tolerate the end of Judaism, etc. (Some may say a Christian regime could tolerate its end, if its leaders became convinced of its falseness; if so, the same would be true for a regime of toleration.)

So why is a regime of toleration important? Why is toleration valuable?

7
General Defenses of Toleration

In the contemporary Western context, there is something decidedly odd about arguments that toleration is a value – because no one really disputes the claim. Most of us think it is a *dependent* value – which is to say that its value is dependent on something else – but we all agree it is of value. Those who think interference in a particular case is permissible simply think the normative limits of toleration have been transgressed. This is largely true even outside the contemporary West. Those ruling theocratic states might claim the US is the "great Satan," intolerably tempting their youth away from the path of righteousness, but they do not say merely "we should not tolerate." The former claim, rather, is a claim that the limits of toleration are transgressed when Western culture infiltrates their own or when Western vices are imported into their homes (likely a form of legal moralism). Just as Pierre Bayle and others thought having differential taxation and not allowing public churches or marches of non-approved religions was consistent with toleration, so no one thinks her own activities intolerant. This, of course, is why getting clear on the definition of toleration – as necessarily including noninterference – is crucial. Differential taxation is a form of interference as it clearly hinders some groups (those taxed more) and helps others (those taxed less), encouraging individuals to move from one to the other. The former group may overcome the hindrance and maintain its membership, but we do not say toleration is *noninterference or interference that is overcomeable*. Toleration is necessarily noninterference.

Importantly, we *should not* tolerate everything. We all believe – correctly – that there are things that should not be tolerated. So why argue for toleration generally? What is important is that we tolerate when we should and do not when we should not. That is why we need good arguments regarding the normative limits of toleration (chapters 3 through 6). Those arguments – and the principles they support – are for toleration of some types of things and against tolera- tion of other types of things. An argument that we should *always* tolerate – no matter what the situation – would be morally deficient. Nonetheless, there is very good reason to discuss at least some of the arguments for general toleration: they are historically important, whether because in the long history of thought about toleration they played an important role in the development of ideas, or, very differently, because at some point they played an historically important role in people's lives. In both cases, it remains an open question whether the arguments are sound. If they are, of course, they must be somewhat circumscribed so that they do not argue for toleration of everything. I shall say that they are argu- ments for *regimes of toleration*, where that should be under- stood to be a regime that accepts good arguments about what should be tolerated – that is, proper normative principles of toleration.

It seems that what matters is defense of a view about what should be tolerated – the discussion of chapters 3 through 6. Absent good countervailing arguments, we should uphold the principles we defend – though they likely require that we remain open to further debate. (Perhaps *that* is the biggest paradox we face.) With that rather large caveat, we turn to several of the standard arguments for general toleration.

The arguments below that work take the form "If you care about X, you should care about toleration because. . . ." This structure is due to toleration being a dependent value, as indicated above. The Xs considered in the sections that follow – those valuable things which make toleration valuable – are (A) conscience or autonomy, (B) rationality or moral personhood, (C) religious belief or salvation, (D) knowledge and truth-acquisition, (F) pursuing your own projects, (G) societal progress, and (H) diversity. There are other arguments that we can't consider here. Some would defend toleration on the grounds that widespread toleration of religions leads to more people taking part in religious activities, thus strengthening religious communities; still others claim it promotes equal respect and peace. I do not think such arguments are necessarily unsound. I do think the arguments just mentioned give us reason to favor toleration. I also discuss, though, two arguments – those from relativism and skepticism (in section E) – that I do not think are sound. These are worth discussing because of their apparent popularity in contemporary culture, though neither argument carries any real weight, as we shall see.

A The arguments from conscience and autonomy

Historically, the most important argument for toleration, at least pre-liberal theory, is almost certainly the religious argument that Augustine offers and that Bayle, Locke, and others sought to improve upon. I'll discuss that argument further in section C below. A component of that argument, at least as formulated by Bayle, is the belief that it is important that people be able to act according to their own conscience. I take this to be fairly uncontroversial; it clearly remains important today. Consider Conscientious Conner. Conner does not consider why he thinks what he does; he is quite comfortable in his religious group and does as he has been taught to do because that is what he believes is right, though he does not consider why he thinks this.

Let's say Conner lives in Reignland under King Feris's rule as a member of the minority religious group discussed in chapter 2, the Quinwanians (remember that they believe they must grow and use quinoa as a staple in their diet). King Feris wants more uniform agriculture than had been present before and so passes a decree that only allows wheat and corn to be planted, grown, harvested, or eaten. Conner, like other

Quinwanians, defies this order and grows quinoa. As time goes by, he is arrested and forced to replace his crops with corn. Feris will not tolerate quinoa-raising. Conner believes this is sacrilegious. Under the ever-watching eyes of Feris's militia, he raises corn, but has lost all semblance of psychological well-being. He constantly worries that God will punish him and that he is damning his family and friends. These worries (and more) wear on him and he grows physically ill. Unable to live according to his beliefs, he suffers. His interests are set back. It would seem they are set back wrongly. Feris's actions against Conner and other Quinwanians are unjustified by any normative principle of toleration that can itself be justified. In any case, I assume we will all agree that there is something very wrong with preventing Conner – and anyone – from living according to their conscience, at least when that involves no harm to others. We can say, then, that *toleration is important because it leaves people free to live according to their conscience*, which often frees them from much psychological distress.

As important as freedom of conscience is, political philosophers today more often make the above sort of case from a concern with autonomy instead. This is to be expected given the philosopher's concern with reason and rationality. Being able to thoroughly reason through a set of choices and adopt the option that reason indicates requires independence from others that might exercise any authority over one's choosing. Conner does not do this – he reasons, but he reasons from a set of precepts learned from others and accepted as authoritative. Put differently, his reasoning is constrained by his dependence on his religious group's beliefs. Philosophers, rightly or wrongly, think we can reason in a less constrained way, at least to be able to judge the options available – this, importantly, is what is needed for genuine autonomy. Acting with autonomy requires thinking through one's available options – and doing so in a way that one is not being led to a certain choice by outside influences. I think this is possible and that a great many of us actually strive – sometimes successfully – to choose autonomously, though this is a more difficult process than acting according to one's conscience. One might never question one's conscience after all. (Notice that, as indicated in chapter 6C, forcing Conner to act *autonomously against his conscience* can be harmful.)

We saw, in chapter 4D, why autonomy is intrinsically valuable. To rehearse the point, imagine that you wake up to go to the park and, after getting ready, you gather your gear and go. Now imagine a parallel scenario where everything is the same except that when you go out to your car, you are chloroformed, kidnapped, and later released right next to your car, which an associate of the kidnapper moved to the park, and that you have been given a drug that makes you forget what happened. You then think, "Wow, I don't remember coming here," but go on into the park. We cringe at the second scenario even though you are not physically or mentally injured and get exactly what you want. Indeed, your actions, however limited they might be, are fully in accord with your conscience. The only difference between the two scenarios is that in the first you act autonomously while in the second you act non-autonomously. That the outcome is the same but we still vastly prefer the first to the second suggests that we value autonomy for its own sake and not just because it is often instrumentally valuable (see Cohen 2004b).

The connection between autonomy and toleration is as straightforward as that between freedom of conscience and toleration. Autonomous agents engage in various and sometimes questionable ways of living – that is, ways of living that others might oppose and that they might wish to interfere with. (Just as there may be opposition to letting Conner live according to his conscience.) Given the value of autonomy, toleration must be adopted to prevent unnecessary interference. (Some, such as Joseph Raz (1986), also suggest that autonomy requires the presence of a range of options to choose from and that such a variety would only exist in an atmosphere of toleration.) Admittedly, the relationship between toleration, on the one hand, and autonomy (or conscience), on the other, is contingent; there may be some utopian world wherein no one opposes any one else or is not tempted to interfere, so that toleration is not needed. In *our* world, though, *toleration is valuable as it leaves us able to act in accord with our conscience; indeed, it leaves us able to do so autonomously if we wish.*

B   The argument for moral muscles

Perhaps the most important argument for toleration from John Stuart Mill – from whom I take the harm principle – is what Joel Feinberg calls the "moral muscles" argument (1986: 384, n.5). Mill tells us that by merely accepting the judgments of those around us instead of considering a situation rationally, we allow our rational faculties to atrophy. Much as an individual loses the use of his legs if he does not exercise them for an extended period of time, an individual who does not exercise her rational abilities can lose them. "The mental and moral, like the muscular, powers are improved only by being used;" if they are not exercised, they become "withered and starved" (Mill 1978[1859]: 56 and 58). Such a loss is far worse than losing one's legs however; without reason, one is not a *moral* being, not a *person*. Given that, we must allow and even encourage the development of reason.

What would encourage the development of reason? How would this "muscle" be exercised? What is necessary is that people think through their available options on their own, not merely accepting what others say. With Mill, I suggest that this is more likely to occur when they are faced with opposing views. If one is faced with opposing possible answers to a question and is unwilling to accept any without thinking it through, then think it through one will – and that is exercising reason. Regimes of toleration provide substantial opportunity for individuals to be in situations like this because in such regimes, opposing views are aired about controversial topics and no one is endorsed as an authority about them. Indeed, the more that is tolerated, the more likely it is that people will be exposed to a variety of views – sometimes disruptively. In facing the challenges posed in such situations, individuals are encouraged (perhaps forced) to think through their beliefs, thus exercising their rational faculties. Sometimes the challenges are not just to decide between new competing views, but challenges to our own fundamental beliefs by views competing directly with them. This should be embraced, though, as, without such challenges, we might complacently accept beliefs handed down to us. "It is when we are confronted with quite radically different forms of life that we are moved to reflect upon the underlying sets of concerns which account for our judgments, actions and beliefs" (Weinstock 1994: 186). Such reflection is the exercise of our reason.

The connection to toleration should now be clear: (a) one is more likely to reason through options if there are challenges to standard beliefs, if there are no standard beliefs but only competing beliefs, and, especially, if one's own beliefs are challenged; and (b) this suggests we should allow people to express different views – we ought to tolerate. *Toleration is useful as a means of allowing competing beliefs, which encourages people to exercise and thus develop their own reason* (cf. Feinberg 1986: 384, n. 5). As reason is often seen (certainly it is seen this way by Mill) as a defining characteristic of personhood or humanity, *toleration is instrumentally valuable for maintaining (and increasing) one's humanity.* This is powerful reason to endorse toleration.

It might be objected that even if some scope of toleration is helpful for allowing challenges to one's views so that one has to exercise one's rational faculties, that scope may be limited. There are four broad possibilities: (1) there is no relationship between facing challenges to one's views and rationality; (2) although such challenges are needed to develop rationality, once any rationality is present, no further challenges are necessary; (3) although some minimal number of challenges are always necessary to maintain rationality, more challenges do not lead to more rationality; and (4) challenges are necessary and more challenges allow for more rationality. Only the first of these is a real threat to the argument as presented. If (2) or (3) were accurate, we would have reason to endorse some toleration (to aid the development of reason where it is not yet present but nonetheless is potentially present, or to help all maintain rationality). Of course, (4) would offer substantial support for my case – and though I will not pursue it here, I do find it intuitively plausible. Admittedly, which of these four is accurate is an empirical question requiring evidence from psychology, but as only the first renders this argument unsound and I think that implausible, I take the argument to have at least some weight.

C   The Augustinian argument, again

As we discussed briefly in chapter 1A (and mentioned again in section A of this chapter), the first historically significant argument for toleration comes from Augustine. That argument, as we saw, had flaws. Various thinkers, though, improved upon Augustine's argument.

Picking up from Augustine's argument, Pierre Bayle argues that human belief about religious questions is necessarily fallible. He believes we can be more certain that persons are owed respect and must have freedom of conscience. Because we can be more sure that persons are owed respect than that our religious beliefs are right (even if we had certitude that God exists, which religion best captures our relation to God would be unclear), we must not interfere with the choices people make regarding religious beliefs and practices. That is, we must tolerate. Alternatively, we might say with Locke, Kant, and Mill that because we can be more sure that individual autonomy is important than that we are correct in our religious beliefs, we must tolerate people acting autonomously, even when that leads them to act in ways we (or our leaders) don't approve. We saw this in section A above, but here feed it back into the Augustinian argument.

Some readers will be surprised that the original Augustinian argument for toleration is unsuccessful. Some readers may wonder about the strength of the Baylean and Lockean/ Millian arguments, questioning how we can have any certainty about the value of freedom of conscience or autonomy. Ultimately, thinkers like Bayle and Locke, both religious thinkers, argue that we have two ways of knowing such things: revelation and reason. (Other thinkers, including Mill, limit themselves to reason.)

On Bayle's view (and, as the reader will know from chapter 1A, Augustine's), only freely accepted belief is satisfactory for salvation. What this means for Bayle, though, is that individuals must come to believe using their own reason. After all, those with reasonable religious faith should be able to recognize that faith is not based on objectively apprehended knowledge (indeed, in one standard view, faith would be unnecessary or even impossible). Once that is recognized, one must admit that fallibility means one might be wrong and others right. So they should be tolerated.[1]

For Bayle, if someone just accepts what his church tells him without reasoning it through himself – even if his acceptance is not forced – he does not have *genuine* belief. Bayle is quite happy to have individuals "rest in the Judgment of the Church" (Bayle 2005[1688]: 74), but only if they get there through reason – that is, only if their conscience leads them to believe the church is correct. Hence, he believes religious believers should endorse the use of reason in order to consult their consciences to see if they can accept the "Judgment of the Church." He also argues that this requires that they not impose their beliefs on others – who must also use reason to consult *their* consciences. Hence, religious believers must tolerate alternative religious views.

It is worth pointing out that the idea that we have more certitude about the importance of conscience or autonomy than we do about religion, and hence must tolerate the acceptance of multiple religions, nicely fits with the harm principle. Mill offers the harm principle partly because he believes we each have a "sphere of action" within which we should be free to do as we like. What goes on inside that "sphere" must be tolerated. That sphere ends where we would harm another in any way. We might add, for the Baylean argument, that the sphere ends where our actions would force someone else to act against her conscience. If the value is autonomy, the sphere ends where another's autonomy would be infringed. As already suggested, both of these are harms.

Locke's basic argument is similar to Bayle's. He claims that "[t]he care . . . of every man's soul belongs unto himself, and is to be left unto himself," and that "[i]f they believe, they will come [to their Church] of their own accord; if they believe not, their coming will nothing avail them" (Locke 1993[1865]: 35, 38). He responds to an objection by advocating noninterference, a key component of toleration:

> But what if he neglect the care of his soul? I answer, what if he neglect the care of his health, or of his estate; which things are nearlier related to the government of the magistrate than the other? Will the magistrate provide by an express law, that

such an one shall not become poor or sick? Laws provide, as much as is possible, that the goods and health of subjects be not injured by the fraud or violence of others; they do not guard them from the negligence or ill husbandry of the possessors themselves. (1993[1865]: 35)[2]

Locke's defense of toleration, like Augustine's and Bayle's,[3] is based on the simple idea that we must not try to force religion on anyone as one *cannot force salvation* on another.[4] To save one's soul, it is claimed, one must have faith in God. But being an intensely personal commitment, Locke suggests, this cannot be forced. Others may force one to *behave* in certain ways – performing the sacraments, for example – but cannot force one to behave in that way *due to genuine belief*. That is, one may be forced to go through the motions of faith, but cannot be forced to *have faith*. Action can be compelled; belief cannot. Forcing belief is not possible because we are not capable of (suddenly) choosing what to believe, though one may pretend to believe in order to satisfy non-tolerating others. *Toleration, then, is instrumentally valuable in that it allows for genuine religious belief and, hence, salvation.*

There is a clear objection to this: as we discussed in chapter 1A, some who are forced *to act in accordance with belief* seem to come *to have belief*. Indeed, it's a commonplace that if one acts in the ways that a believer acts, one may, in time, find oneself believing. There may well be a psychological mechanism that takes one from feigned belief to genuine belief. If that is the case, then perhaps one can be forced to have faith by *indirect* means, thereby saving one's soul. Perhaps, as Augustine came to think, by forcing a non-believer to act as a believer acts, one can indirectly help the non-believer become a believer.[5]

A partial defense is possible here. When Augustine witnessed the elimination of the Donatist heresy, it was not likely because all of those who had previously accepted it were genuinely transformed and thus refuted the purported heresy. More likely, the "heretics" were simply not allowed to "corrupt" anyone else with their teachings. Some may have rejected the supposed heresy, others may have pretended to reject it, but just as likely, some who did neither were killed and, importantly, *none was allowed to preach*. Some of those who pretended to refute the heresy may have come not to believe it and to accept the orthodox view, but it's not clear they all did. Even if they did not, given that none could preach and some were killed, the result was as one would expect: the sect was unable to propagate. If the purpose in persecution is to save souls and saving souls is accomplished by having people accept strict Roman Catholicism, it was likely successful in one way and a failure in another. Given no knowledge of the heresy, fewer people would be "corrupted" and thus more would accept the orthodox view (and thus, perhaps, be able to attain salvation). On the other hand, some of those who were already "corrupted" were not saved but killed or relegated to a life of pretense. In either case, from the non-tolerating believers' perspective, they were presumably subject to eternal damnation. If one is a consequentialist (of a fairly unsophisticated sort), this may have been a success, with more saved than damned. As a policy aimed at a "utilitarianism of salvation," persecution can clearly work if carried out carefully. Importantly, though, we have no clear evidence that not tolerating disbelief will always lead to belief, indirectly or otherwise. It may be impossible to force faith upon any given individual (as Locke insists) and yet possible to save more souls by persecuting heretics (as Augustine came to believe).

Is it impossible to force faith on individuals? The answer is not as definitive as we might like. It is true that we often come to believe what we pretend to believe.[6] In some cases, then, where persecution leads people to pretend to believe doctrine, it can be successful – even with regard to those individuals. Some forms of persecution – that is, failures to tolerate – may work. Others may not. What does this say about the (possible) value of toleration? Again, the answer is not as definitive as we might like. We can summarize it by saying that (a) if an advocate of a religion is a utilitarian of salvation, he would rationally not tolerate disbelievers – indeed, would rationally eliminate them as quickly as possible – but (b) if the advocate couples his religious belief with a belief in the sanctity of the individual (or if the religion includes a doctrine of such sanctity), so that he rejects a utilitarianism of salvation, then *only if* he is committed to encouraging religious belief *and* he confidently believes persecution would successfully convert disbelievers *without* violating that sanctity *and without* (accidentally) causing other believers to lose faith, would he rationally not tolerate disbelievers. Of course, it may be difficult or impossible to convert disbelievers without violating others' sanctity or causing others to lose faith. Hence, (c) if one is not committed to encouraging religious belief *or* if one is thus committed but does not confidently believe persecution would successfully convert disbelievers without violating the sanctity of individuals or without (accidentally) causing other believers to lose faith, one should tolerate disbelief.

Importantly, even if the argument from religious salvation fails to fully support toleration, there are other, equally or more persuasive, arguments for toleration. This argument, though, is not without any persuasive value – for religious believers and those who think religious belief is of value.

D   The argument for knowledge and truth-acquisition

On Mill's view, there is a connection between toleration and knowledge. Philosophers define knowledge (roughly) as true justified belief. Though you may believe there are living breathing unicorns of the sort described in fairytales, you cannot *know* there are because there are not. You cannot *know* something that is false. Nor can you know something you have no justification for believing. $1{,}234 \times 1{,}234 = 1{,}522{,}756$, but until you work out the problem (or use a trusted calculator, or . . .) you are not justified in believing it and so cannot *know* it. On Mill's view (see, e.g., Mill 1978[1859]: 35–6), you are only justified in maintaining a belief if you subject it to scrutiny – for holding to a belief without subjecting it to scrutiny allows too easily for dogmatically holding beliefs that should be rejected (and, perhaps, rejecting beliefs that should be held). Dissent and differing ways of life, Mill then argues, must be permitted so that all face opposing views, which will, in turn, encourage the scrutiny of beliefs. When we scrutinize our beliefs, we might discover an error in our thinking. If we do not, we may be justified in our belief and so may have knowledge. *Toleration is thus instrumentally valuable as a means to justification and knowledge.*

Consider my belief that there are no genuine miracles – events that occur counter to the laws of nature. When faced with a religious believer claiming to have witnessed a miracle, I am forced to consider their claim and any evidence they have. If I am intellectually honest, I have to be open to the possibility that I was previously wrong. I thus scrutinize not only their claim and evidence, but also the reasons for my own previous belief (which I may end up keeping or discarding). The long-run hope is that what is justifiably believed – what survives the scrutiny – is in fact true. We will consider truth-acquisition shortly, but first it is worth considering a different argument about epistemic justification.

What should be emphasized in this sort of discussion is that one *cannot* be justified in rejecting a view one does not understand only because one has not considered it. A good (intellectually honest) epistemic agent does not reject a view without considering it. The good epistemic agent – one who can be reliably expected to come to justified belief – rejects views only on justifiable grounds.[7] She might reject the claim that there is a wheel spinning inside her chest that keeps her animated, for example, because she has seen other humans with their chests cut open who had no such wheel. She would not, though, reject the Baha'i faith for example, merely because it was founded in the late nineteenth century and "no real religion could have been founded that late." Given this, if one is to be justified in rejecting any religious (or other) view, one must know about that view. To know about them requires that information about them be available and that requires toleration of the dissemination of that information. In short, it requires toleration of speech.[8]

Now let us consider our ability to acquire (knowledge of) truth. Mill claims that if we do not tolerate dissent, we prohibit the hearing of possibly true propositions. If they are true and successfully prohibited, Mill believes that truth is essentially stolen from those who would otherwise hear it. This is part of his reason for claiming that "If all mankind minus one were of one opinion, mankind would be no more justified in silencing that one person, than he, if he had the power, would be justified in silencing mankind" (Mill 1978[1859]: 16). Importantly, in his view, even if the propositions are false there would be theft – not of the truth, of course, but of the opportunity to clarify the truth (of allowed beliefs) and of the opportunity to develop sincere commitment to those beliefs rather than mere acquiescence. Epistemic acquiescence is problematic because it leaves us susceptible to being convinced by bad arguments. Those who merely acquiesce to a claim rather than scrutinizing it might just as easily acquiesce to the opposite. To prevent theft of truth or the opportunity to clarify the truth and develop sincere commitment, we must endorse a regime of toleration. Hence, "In the face of uncertainty," a recent commentator tells us, "toleration is the only, or the best, way to ensure that the truth emerges"; because we are all fallible, without toleration "we cannot know that a suppressed belief does not embody the truth" (Newey 1999: 127). With toleration, we will be forced to scrutinize our beliefs and are thus more likely to attain truth.

Against those who say toleration is not necessary for truth since truth will always win out, Mill says, "[T]he dictum that truth always triumphs over persecution, is one of those pleasant falsehoods which men repeat after one another till they pass into commonplaces, but which all experience refutes." He adds: "It is a piece of idle sentimentality that truth, merely as truth, has any inherent power denied to error of prevailing against the dungeon and the stake" (1978[1859]: 27, 28). "The real advantage which truth has, consists in this, that when an opinion is true, it may be extinguished once, twice, or many times, but in the course of ages there will generally be found persons to rediscover it, until some one of its reappearances falls on a time when from favorable circumstances it escapes persecution until it has made such head as to withstand all subsequent attempts to suppress it" (1978[1859]: 28). That it will (likely) emerge eventually does not mean it will win out now.

Consider the case of peer review in academic journals. Papers go through a more or less rigorous examination by reviewers and editors who serve as "gate-keepers" refusing to publish poorly constructed or defended pieces.[9] This is as it should be. We do not want the editors of *Nature* to publish the creationist ravings of a random author (assuming they would not be scientifically defended). But this is what I would call a *local* matter – a specific and narrow community of individuals would not hear the view. Given the readership of *Nature*, publishing such an article would be a mistake. This does not mean, though, that we should not tolerate the publication of the article, should the author find a willing publisher. Another publisher, of, say, *Creation and Arts and Science Herald*, might be happy to accept it. Its publication in that journal may well cause some to believe false claims – and this would immediately lower the overall level of truth awareness. But this, again, is a local matter – some members of a specific and narrow community would be misled.[10]

The important question to consider is not local, but *global*: would suppression or toleration of the piece conduce to truth-acquisition in the broadest possible community? While we have to admit that some – perhaps many – individuals do worse because they are misled when the publication of false claims is tolerated, we can still believe that society as a whole does better because more truths are known – indeed, more truths may be known by more people. Mill's point is that by tolerating dissenting views, critical discussion would emerge and more people would learn the truth – i.e., more people in the largest relevant community would acquire truth. At the global level, more truth is acquired. In fact, even some local and perhaps unanticipated communities could benefit. For example, philosophy professors can use the creationist piece in our logic and critical reasoning classes, to teach several truths – truths about logic as well as evolution. All told, even though the amount of falsehoods acquired in one or more localities may increase, the amount of truth acquired in all the various localities put together may well be more than it would be if we simply suppressed the dissenting view. I suspect it would, but I admit I cannot prove this definitively.

While there "is no guarantee that people will actually track the dialectical merits of the countervailing arguments" (Goldman 1999: 212), this means only that there may be a local loss of truth-acquisition. Moreover, there is no guarantee that with any particular regime of global (of special concern, governmental) information gatekeepers, truth-acquisition would be promoted. Of course, fraud and libel

laws are desirable as a means of not tolerating harmful statements of falsehoods about particular products or people, but
much debate is not about such statements. We should be
hesitant to grant any body, governmental or otherwise, the
ability to suppress non-harmful dissenting views based on a
claim that doing so may – or is likely to – increase truth-
acquisition. We do better, I think, to err on the side of caution
by tolerating false speech. *Toleration of dissent promotes
truth acquisition.* (Relating this to the argument of the previous section, the truth that might be acquired with toleration
may be religious in nature. In any case, we should not forget
that what the truth is may surprise us.)

E   The arguments from relativism and skepticism (rejected)

All this talk of reason (from B), justification, knowledge, and
truth (from D) may leave some readers worried. Despite what
I said in chapter 3C, many will instinctively think "all these
are relative; there is no absolute or universal truth." Indeed,
there is a popular argument for toleration in contemporary
(Western) culture that takes this belief in a lack of universality
as its premise. The argument is deceptively simple: as everything is relative, we should not impose our views, so should
tolerate. This argument takes a variety of forms depending
on the sort of relativism being espoused. In one version,
knowledge is thought to be relative to individual knowers.
Call this subjectivism. The subjectivist believes that what is
true for him is not necessarily true for you. According to
cultural relativism, by contrast, knowledge is indexed to cultures so that what is true for one culture is not necessarily
true for another culture. Given that there is nothing that is
universally true, the idea goes, we can't insist on our own
view and so should tolerate. As popular as this argument is,
it is simply misguided.[11] I won't discuss this argument at any
length, but simply point out that if everything is relative, the
idea that "we should tolerate" is also relative. This means
that in the subjectivist view, if I believe it to be true, it's true
for me and I should tolerate, but if you don't, you shouldn't.

Or, on the cultural variant: if my culture believes we should tolerate, we should, but if yours doesn't, it shouldn't. Not exactly a helpful defense of toleration; it ends up being, "Tolerate if you believe you should" – and we should worry about those who do not believe they should. Indeed, why this argument is as popular as it is, is unclear. Why would one believe that we should not impose our views if there is no (objective) truth about not imposing views?

One suggestion is that it's normal in our society both to *want to* tolerate and to think that if we can judge others and their beliefs we will be in a position not to tolerate them if they are somehow judged less good than us. Given these competing factors, it might be natural to think: "Well, I guess since I should tolerate, I should not judge others – so their views must have as much validity as mine." But this is a mistake. What we should think is: "Since I should tolerate, I should not interfere with them, *even if I judge them to be wrong or bad.*" Indeed, if the noninterference is to be genuine toleration – thinking back now to chapter 1B – I must judge them in some way, whether morally or otherwise. I can only tolerate what I oppose. I would suggest, in fact, that it is natural and wise to judge others (as already suggested in the introductory section of chapter 1) and less natural but often wiser still to tolerate those one judges wrong.

It is worth pointing out another view that claims not that truth is relative, but that it is impossible for us to know if what we believe is true. This is skepticism, a viable and classic philosophical view. (David Hume is often thought of as a skeptic, for example.) Skepticism also has different forms, the broadest being *global* skepticism – the view that we cannot be certain that any belief is true. A more limited skepticism is what we can call normative skepticism – the view that we cannot be certain that any normative belief (whether about aesthetics, morality, or political life) is true. The argument for toleration from either of these claims parallels that from relativism: since we cannot know if our beliefs or yours are true, we should not impose our beliefs on you so should tolerate. While I am sympathetic to the skeptic, the argument from skepticism to toleration is weak. If we cannot be certain that our beliefs are true, we cannot be certain our belief that toleration is good is true.

Global skepticism is untenable. It cannot rationally be doubted that a triangle has three sides. It may be that there are no triangles or no triangular things, but anything that is a triangle has three sides. More generally, while we can doubt all empirical claims, we cannot rationally doubt any tautologies (*P is P*, after all). What might matter for us, though, is whether normative skepticism holds or if there are any normative claims that cannot be doubted. Here I think it is important that there is no clear line between the normative and the non-normative. For example, the proposition that "suffering is bad" seems to be conceptual; badness is built into the definition of "suffering." Moreover, it's also a conceptual point that, all other things equal, badness should be avoided. The normative conclusion that all other things equal, we should avoid suffering, follows immediately. The remaining question is simply whether we can doubt that we should tolerate – or should tolerate unless there is harm. I do not doubt that we can – which is why I think the argument from skepticism to toleration is weak. So we will continue.

In my view, we can and should remain *healthily skeptical*, recognizing that our views – including our view that toleration is important – may be wrong but continue to hold to them until we have good reason not to. We can hold to them without being dogmatic, as indicated in the last section. We can do so willing to consider counter-arguments.

What skeptics and relativists have in common is a belief that we cannot know of any claim that it is true for all epistemic beings in all contexts. This belief often itself hinges on a recognition that we are fallible.[12] Human beings are, it is (correctly) thought, inherently fallible beings.

Fallibilism is the view that, as fallible epistemic beings, our knowledge is always potentially mistaken. This provides something of an explanation for skepticism – i.e., it says: "We should be skeptical of ever really knowing because we are fallible – we know that we have been wrong before and will be wrong again." Fallibilism sometimes leads skeptics and relativists to endorse toleration. Given that anyone may be wrong about the epistemic status and hence value of any particular belief that might be suppressed, there is prima facie reason to forgo suppression and to tolerate. We should fear eliminating anything of value.

I take fallibilism itself to have much merit – as I do skepticism (though not relativism). It is, though, of decidedly limited use for a defense of toleration by skeptics and relativists. The skeptic can insist that we should tolerate, but cannot insist we can *know* we should tolerate. While that may be enough for those unconcerned with justification, it is a weak claim: "I think we should tolerate, but I am fallible and may be wrong."[13] The relativist fares worse: as we've seen, he can only claim that toleration is a value to him or his culture so he or it should tolerate. He might use fallibilism as an *explanation* for his relativism, but it does not help with a defense of toleration. Neither skepticism nor relativism can support toleration.

Recognizing our fallibility means we should recognize that we might be wrong about the value of toleration – which I nonetheless defend. This does not mean the project here is fundamentally misguided any more than any scientific inquiry is misguided. The best scientists pursue knowledge recognizing they might make a mistake in that pursuit. So too philosophers.

As I cannot argue against fallibilism or even skepticism, I would simply encourage recognition of our fallibility and then continuation with the project. Importantly, fallibilism is consistent with believing that one is not wrong now, so that one puts forward one's view (about toleration or anything else) *as if* it were true, but with a willingness to be corrected – as I've already several times suggested. This, it seems to me, is the correct stance for any philosopher or scientist.[14] Moreover, toleration occupies a strange position here as it can be instrumental in helping us attain truth and knowledge *despite our fallibility*, as discussed in section D above.

F   The argument for project pursuit

Another argument for toleration concerns what philosophers call "project pursuit." Persons generally have projects they wish to pursue – projects that likely improve their lives. These can be short term, but it often seems that we need long-term projects to have a truly worthwhile life. Recent political philosophers as diverse as John Rawls, Loren Lomasky, and Alasdair MacIntyre have all recognized the importance of project pursuit. Without something we are trying to accomplish – perhaps writing the Great American Novel, raising good children, building a successful business, or defending toleration – there seems little point in living. Importantly for us, we may find ourselves doubting the "point" of life if we are continually and systematically frustrated in our attempts to pursue our projects to the extent that we come to believe the tasks impossible. It seems clear that as we (usually) have more intimate knowledge of our projects than others, we are more likely to achieve our projects when we are free to choose what we do – when we are tolerated. We are more likely to make choices that aid our project pursuit than others are – even well-meaning others. "Speaking generally, there is no one so fit to conduct any business, or to determine how or by whom it shall be conducted, as those who are personally interested in it" (Mill 1978[1859]: 107).[15] Toleration, which allows us to make our own choices when others oppose those choices is, then, *instrumentally valuable to the pursuit of projects*. People ought to be tolerated so they can pursue their own projects.

Some doubt the claim that all people have their own projects. If projects must be autonomously chosen, then I would also doubt the claim. However, it seems likely that there can be non-autonomously chosen projects. It might be the project of an individual to "follow the dream" of their religious leaders (where the dream is thought to be a vision provided by the deity) or to simply follow some charismatic leader.[16] The project is what the person must act on in order to follow her own conscience. That may be something autonomously chosen or not.

I should make clear that this argument is very different from the argument about autonomy in section A above. That argument requires that autonomy is a value; this argument assumes only that the pursuit, and perhaps – but not necessarily – successful completion of one's projects, is a value. As just suggested, one can have, and successfully complete, projects without autonomy. Of course, it's also true that one can autonomously fail to complete one's projects. Hence the two values – autonomy and project pursuit – are distinct. Toleration is instrumentally valuable as a means to both. Sometimes they will coincide, but they are distinct nonetheless.

G   The argument for societal progress

We return, one last time, to Mill (1978[1859]: 61–7). This argument[17] begins by noting that tolerating individuals' non-standard behaviors (consider the Wright brothers' first flight, which many would have thought crazy) allows them the opportunity to develop new and better ways to perform daily tasks and, thus, to develop new and better ways of life, typically while engaging in a project they think valuable. Indeed, toleration makes possible the existence of geniuses, as discussed in 4D.

To rehearse the argument: geniuses are unique, and if they are forced to do as others insist – if their eccentricities are not tolerated – their creativity would likely be stifled and this would lessen the innovation and progress in society. Put more simply, if no individual (genius or not) is permitted to choose against societal norms, we would not gain new technologies or improved ways to live. Toleration, then, is instrumentally valuable *as a means to allowing geniuses to thrive, and partially through them, encouraging innovation and progress*. By allowing individuals to choose on their own, we allow them the opportunity to develop new and better ways of performing daily tasks and to develop new and better ways of life.[18]

The argument here may seem to be only about the instrumental value of toleration of (or at least noninterference with) those who would be geniuses. Worse, it might be thought only to provide *them* a reason to value toleration. Both suggestions are myopic. First, many people innovate, coming up with improvements that help us all, not just geniuses. Second, everyone in society benefits from the innovation such individuals (genius or not) develop, so all have reason to tolerate. Third, because we cannot know in advance who will be a genius or innovator and because such individuals may be anyone born into any segment of society, we have reason to tolerate all. Fourth, having a social environment in which people are tolerated is likely to encourage more individuals to become geniuses or to otherwise innovate – another Millian point (see Mill 1978[1859]: 62). So long as we think there is a possibility of improving anything, we all have reason to want innovation – and innovators – tolerated. So long as we can't know who will innovate (or suspect that toleration encourages more innovation), we have reason to want all tolerated.

The innovations that can emerge in a regime of toleration can benefit everyone and since we cannot know who will develop them, we should have extensive toleration of differences so that society can improve. The hope is that most will see the instrumental value of allowing others the freedom to develop different, sometimes better, ways to live. Those that are committed to traditional ways of life and who see innovation as threatening what they cherish will not be persuaded, of course, but here's a point that is too often missed: they too would be tolerated! Those who want a traditional way of life with strict rules and strong community bonds would be free to live their lives as they see fit if society took toleration as seriously as I suggest it should and endorsed the strict version of the harm principle. As Gillian Brock indicates, "[t]he basic freedoms [afforded by a regime of toleration] are useful to everyone, even those who might prefer lives that place little emphasis on the value of individual freedom and choice," even those in "cultures that value obedience to tradition, respect for elders' authority, subservience of personal freedoms for the good of the culture, and so forth" (2009: 154). Individuals wanting such cultural groups are free to have them so long as others also want them. They could not, of course, force others to stay in their cultural group or join a new one, but they could join with like-minded individuals to live as they wish.

H   The arguments for pluralism and diversity

"Pluralism" and "diversity" are ideas often associated with toleration. It's worth considering both, though I do not think the first gives toleration any support.

Many liberals accept some form of moral pluralism: the view that there are irreducibly plural moral values. For such thinkers, toleration may be thought useful as a means of allowing the multiple values to coexist. This is contingent, however, on it being the case that none of the multiple values requires interfering with, rather than tolerating, activity performed in the name of one of the other values.

Consider that advocates of the value of religious commitment (regardless of the religion), may favor not tolerating atheism, even when autonomously chosen. On the other side, advocates of the value of autonomy favor not tolerating autonomy-inhibiting behaviors that might be associated with religious commitment (as opposed to what I say in chapter 6C). Clearly, the values of religious commitment and autonomy can conflict, each requiring interference with acts performed for the other. This is not necessarily a problem for either the religious or the promoter of autonomy. It is, though, a problem for the pluralist – for if the pluralist's goal is to endorse the existence and recognition of plural values, this may require stifling, rather than tolerating, activity aimed at convincing people that one or more of the endorsed values is not a value. Pluralism, then, would seem to require toleration on some fronts, but not others. This is not an argument in favor of general toleration, but in favor of toleration of particular values and their pursuit – perhaps all, but only, the values that do not involve the sort of conflict that might exist between the religious advocate and the promoter of autonomy. Recognition that there are plural values does not then provide a general argument for toleration.[19] Such an argument is more plausibly derived, though, from the political view that sees diversity as a value (the diversity need not be of moral values).[20]

When we tolerate, as we saw above in section A, people can act autonomously. That, in turn, makes it likely that diverse ways of life will form. Put differently, when we tolerate people acting autonomously, it's likely that they will live their lives in diverse ways. The reverse also holds: if we do not tolerate autonomy, but require everyone to live the same way, we are unlikely to get diversity. Hence, it seems that if one values diversity, one should value toleration. This may not seem the strongest sort of argument available, as the value of diversity is itself in need of defense. However, I think the prevalence in contemporary discourse of the value of diversity – particularly of the multicultural variety – has much merit, so I think this argument has some weight. Let us consider the advocate of a diversity of cultures.

Multiculturalists often want cultural diversity encouraged. We cannot, though, say simply that if diversity is a value, toleration is a value. An advocate of X, as we saw in chapter 1B, does not tolerate X because they cannot (conceptually) – to tolerate requires opposing, not advocating. The advocate of diversity thus cannot tolerate it, though she can accept or encourage it. In the process, though, she can encourage others to tolerate the diversity – and she can tolerate some element of the diversity that she opposes and can encourage others to do the same. For example, she might think living with diverse cultures is great even though she personally dislikes the French culture; this leaves her able to tolerate French culture and to advocate that others tolerate all cultures they dislike. Hence, *if diversity is a value and there are any that oppose some element of the valued diversity, toleration is valuable as a means to allowing the diversity despite opposition.*

Interestingly, if everyone in a society chose to live his or her life in the same (non-diverse) way, toleration would not result in diversity. If it's diversity that is the value, toleration would be abandoned in such circumstances in favor of interference to create and maintain diversity – such interference may involve subsidizing (perhaps via tax breaks) minorities, for example. In such cases, the advocate of diversity will also be an advocate of non-toleration. So the argument from diversity is somewhat limited. The limitation, thus framed, might rightly be considered minor, since there is, in our society and every known human society, both diversity and some elements that oppose other elements of that diversity. Hence, it might be thought, toleration is a value in every human society even if it might not be a value in a non-diverse utopia.

Typically, of course, we do not value diversity of all possible belief systems or cultures. Most of us are quite happy to see the end of Nazi culture, for example. Still, other cultures we admire may come to an end. That is, even in real societies, it may happen that all those committed to a particular belief system slowly and voluntarily cease to accept that belief system. When the few remaining Shakers, for example, die, there will be no more Shakers. Some might think: "Well, advocating diversity does not mean advocating for all existing elements of an existing diversity." Such thinkers – reasonable, in my view – might continue to be advocates of toleration by those who oppose *other* components of the existing diversity of cultural groups without supporting activity to encourage a Shaker revival. Indeed, as already noted, protecting all elements of an existing diversity will require activity that is not toleration – perhaps subsidizing potential initiates into dying belief systems, for example. Those who can and do advocate toleration – both of existing cultures and of the dying of some of those cultures – can point out that while it is natural and acceptable for some elements of an existing diversity to disappear, new ones will appear, replenishing the diversity. The argument from diversity thus seems to have some merit.

Some have a real worry that more and more elements of an existing diversity can disappear, so that genuine diversity ceases to exist and a "monoculture" remains. As Tyler Cowen (2002) has shown, what would really happen in such a situation is that the single culture that would emerge (or *is emerging*) would contain elements of all the cultures that have ceased to exist as distinct cultures. This would be an end to diversity in one sense – there would not be multiple distinct cultural groups. But it would be a continuation of diversity in another sense – the monoculture that emerged would have tremendous diversity within it with different sorts of music, visual arts, theater, etc. This would not be the mock diversity on display at Disney's Epcot Center, but a real diversity where any particular individual might have Asian or African art hanging in her home, enjoy Peruvian or Tibetin food, etc.

There is a different way of looking at diversity – not a concern directly with cultures, but simply with the fact that different people have different interests and abilities. With this sort of diversity – which is sometimes indirectly linked to differences in cultures – we have greater division of labor and greater production of goods and services that might have value. More simply, with diversity – at least where it is accompanied by tolerant attitudes – we have production of great wealth. As Muldoon et al. (2012) argue, we all gain, materially, when we trade with others; we gain more when we trade with more others; we gain still more when we trade with more diverse others (who presumably have different skill sets). Given these simple facts, we do well – that is, it is in our self-interest – to tolerate as many others as possible so that we can trade (and trade well) with them. Strictly speaking, our noninterference in such cases may not be toleration – because we don't oppose the others and because our reason for noninterference seems not to be principled. Still, we can advocate that others tolerate those they oppose so that we can all prosper (a principled reason)[21] – as suggested by the argument for societal progress, discussed in the previous section. Such toleration seems clearly important as it helps us all flourish (materially).

We can now say fairly definitively, I think, that toleration is a value. We cannot say, of course, that we should tolerate everything all the time. Earlier chapters discussed various principles that purport to show when toleration is properly called for and when it is not. As I've indicated, I think defense of the correct set of those principles is our most important task. As also indicated, I favor a strict version of the harm principle and rejection of the others though I would not claim that the arguments I have provided on that score are definitive (at least not all of them). The arguments in this chapter may also not be completely definitive, but they do seem to me jointly (extremely) persuasive. And there are others. But we move on, approaching the end of this investigation.

8
Conclusion

A Recognizing we want to be tolerated

My discussion, in the last chapter, of the arguments for toleration is incomplete in that there are other arguments for toleration that I do not discuss. The arguments discussed were chosen because of their intuitive appeal, popularity, or cogency. My discussion there is also incomplete in that I avoid a variety of intricacies of each of the arguments presented. Fully exploring all of those in a book of this sort would be impossible. Despite the incompleteness, it should be clear that several of the arguments I discuss – those having to do with freedom of conscience, autonomy, reason, and project pursuit – are meant to be universal. My claim is that no matter who you are, you have a vested interest in being tolerated so that you can live according to your conscience, choose autonomously, be respected, develop (or maintain) your rational capacity, and determine and pursue your own projects. I also think all should endorse the increased acquisition of justified belief and knowledge and increases in societal progress that toleration allows, though I realize those committed to more traditional cultural values may oppose them and some of the others (wrongly, in my view). Without toleration, all this (and more) would be at risk.

Mill tells us that allowing a government the power to limit choice – to not tolerate – adds unnecessarily to the government's power and so should be avoided – presumably because a government strong enough to prevent us from making bad choices is strong enough to prevent us from making good choices (Mill 1978[1859]: 108). Put simply, we have reason to want to limit government power – not for the sake of limiting government, but because it is better for us if government is limited, as then we can act on conscience, perhaps autonomously, and pursue our projects as we like, etc. Indeed, we have reason to want to limit *any* accumulated power, for any accumulated power can be used against us as well as for us. What this means is that we should not want any individual or group, governmental otherwise, to fail to tolerate non-harmful activity of others when such failure can result in dangerously increased power. We want to have a government (for example) that tolerates much simply because we do not want to give it the power not to tolerate – in part for fear that it may unfairly and unnecessarily fail to tolerate us. We want toleration, in part, because we do not want anyone, governmentally or not, to interfere with us. We want to be able to act as we wish.[1]

Consider: if George claims we should not value toleration, it is likely that *he* wants not to tolerate others and wants *us* to aid him in the process. If he wants actively not to tolerate others, he wants to suppress or change them and likely wants our help in doing so. Of course, he will surely want *his* way of life tolerated. That is, he values toleration *of him*. We all want our own ways to be tolerated (if opposed). Neither George nor anyone else would claim otherwise.

The point of this simple example is that it is unfortunate that political commentators, theorists, and philosophers often talk of toleration as something granted to others, without acknowledging that they want their own ways of life tolerated. One exception to this is T. M. Scanlon, who tells us: "I am content to leave others to the religious practices of their choice provided that they leave me free to enjoy none" (1996: 230). Most of us, though, assume that no one would have any reason to want to eliminate *our* way of life. This is an egocentric and dangerous assumption. One reason we should all value toleration is that we each want to be tolerated

ourselves.[2] There is a "value we place on authenticity as one
of life's fundamental goods. We want a sense that we are the
authors of our own lives, that our lives, if you will, are stories
that we write rather than just read" (Mills 1998: 163). If we
are to author our own lives, we must be tolerated (or at least
not interfered with). Recognizing this may help spur a hopefully resounding rejection of the significance of the desire of
some individuals or groups to be free not to tolerate others.
This is "the substantive heart of liberalism" (Hampton 1989:
811): the belief that my way of life – and yours – *must* be
tolerated so long as it does not involve us harming others
against their will, regardless of what anyone else thinks of
the way of life in question. This means that any individual's
desire not to tolerate my (harmless to others) behavior warrants no political merit and it means that even if you wish to
develop a community in which autonomy is not valued, I
must tolerate your choice – provided you do not develop that
community by coercing others to join (hence not tolerating
their choices).

It is of the utmost importance, then, that you not think of
toleration as only about other people. It is too easy to conclude that toleration is not warranted when thinking about
whether someone else (or their behavior or belief) should be
tolerated. We must remember that toleration is important to
us because someone might think *our* ways of life should not
be tolerated. If we want our ways of life to be tolerated, we
should be prepared to defend toleration in general. This is
not merely a matter of intellectual consistency – though it is
that; it is a matter of practical urgency. One cannot consistently claim that their own idiosyncrasies must be tolerated
but their neighbor's need not be. If there is a difference, that
difference must be made plain. We should do so, of course,
by defending definite normative principles of toleration. (E.g.,
the harm principle.) Then, when we say Sue ought to be tolerated but Seth ought not be tolerated, we can do so with
consistency and clarity of reason. Moreover, we can expect
that others will use our claims for their own purposes – if I
argue that Seth ought not be tolerated because he offends me,
I can expect that someone (e.g., Seth) will claim I ought not
be tolerated because I offend them. I should thus be careful
with what I say to justify ending toleration. I am prepared to

say that no one ought to be tolerated when they seek to harm me or my loved ones and I am equally prepared to say that I ought not be tolerated if I seek to harm others.

Toleration, on the view defended here, is *not* one-sided in the way it was considered in its earlier incarnations (see chapter 1A); the ideal is *mutual or reciprocal* toleration. We not only prefer life under King Juris to life under King Feris, we also prefer a life with no king at all – we prefer a life where no one gets to decide unilaterally whether we are tolerated while we get no say in whether they are tolerated. We want to be tolerated and we should want to tolerate others. I am prepared to tolerate everyone and their behaviors so long as they do no harm. This does not mean, of course, that I like – much less, love, as we shall see below – them. Indeed, if I did, I could not (conceptually) tolerate them. I do not expect everyone to like (or love) me. I do expect everyone to tolerate me – so long as I do no harm.

B Toleration as *the* political value

You should now have a view about what toleration is, why it is a value, and when it is called for. Of course, there may be remaining disagreements about any of these. Importantly, given firmer understanding of what toleration is, there may be disagreement with my defense (or rejection) of one or more of the arguments for toleration. Even more importantly, I hope you are now able to develop other arguments on your own (or recognize such arguments in other writings).

Most importantly, from my point of view, given firmer understanding of what toleration is and why it is a value, you may disagree with my views about when it is and is not warranted. You may not accept that the harm principle is the only correct normative principle of toleration. You may find yourself thinking Feinberg is right that there are some offenses that are not harms but warrant interference (endorsing the offense principle). You may find yourself thinking that the provision of certain benefits to those in need who are nonetheless not harmed warrants some interference (endorsing the benefit to others principle). You may even come to believe that interferences can sometimes be justified on paternalist or moralist grounds (endorsing either legal paternalism or legal moralism). My hope is that you are in a better position to argue with others about toleration than if you merely memorized what is written in this book.

To conclude, let's briefly discuss why toleration is sometimes thought (correctly) to be an *unfortunate* virtue of liberal societies. It is needed after all, because there is opposition. Many claim it would be better if citizens of liberal societies did not oppose those who were different from them. Some even claim that it would be better if we embraced those who were different. Surely, there is something right about this. But there is also something wrong with it. A society wherein there is "universal love" would not be a recognizably human society and would not be a society in which love for one's family and friends *mattered*. If one loves everyone, than one's love for one's family is not special. If one has *special* relationships that are essentially characterized by love, then one does not love everyone (at least not in the same way).

Toleration *is* an unfortunate virtue. This is not because universal love is better. It is because *indifference to many and caring for a few* is better. Toleration is needed because people tend to oppose some of the others with whom they are not in a special relationship (and even some with whom they are in such a relationship). It would be better, I suggest, if they were simply indifferent to those others. But that too is utopian. Imagine a world – a genuine utopia – wherein people loved a few, hated no one, and were indifferent to the rest of the people. In such a world, people would have close friends and family whom they would, I assume, seek to help. They would seek to help, though, in fully respectful and, perhaps, loving ways. No one would seek to interfere with a loved one in any way that the loved one would find intrusive. It would only be welcome help (consented to). As for the rest of the world, no one would seek to interfere with them because they would be indifferent to them. No one would (consciously or subconsciously) think better of himself or herself by watching others fail. No one would want any of those others to fail – because one would not think of those others. That is what genuine indifference amounts to. Such a world is utopian. At least it is in my view. I imagine some will think it dystopian – a horrible place where almost no one watches *The Housewives of LA/NJ/NY* or any other reality show. Such shows are not likely to be entertaining if you don't care about any of the reality "stars." The only fans would be friends and family. Whether this is utopian or dystopian, at the end of the day, does not matter. It's not a world we have any hope of attaining.

Universal indifference to all but friends and family is not forthcoming. Nor, of course, is universal love. We must make do with toleration. Of course, we must make do with a proper understanding of toleration, its value, and what it requires. I hope that this book has helped in that regard. Even if there are errors – as there are sure to be – I hope you are in a better position to argue intelligently with others (myself included) about toleration than if you merely memorized what I wrote. That was my goal in writing it.

Notes

Chapter 1   The Topic and Its Historical Relevance

1   The historical record here is somewhat less clear even than I
    indicate. It may be, in fact, that Spinoza wanted the excom-
    munication, as it would rid him of the debts he inherited from
    his father. This would not, though, affect the fact that the
    Jewish community failed to tolerate him – it would simply
    mean he took advantage of the fact that the community would
    not tolerate him. For an interesting discussion, see Nadler
    1999: 116ff.
2   Galeotti is concerned with the "symbolic meaning" of tolera-
    tion (for one helpful explanation, see Galeotti 2002: 100–1;
    for some defense of that approach, see 2002: 87–95).

Chapter 2   Two Approaches to the Normative Issues

1   Actually many political philosophers actually did both, but
    there is a strong tendency amongst political philosophers to
    view the two projects as distinct.
2   We won't here be concerned with what the different ground-
    ings were for these thinkers.
3   To continue the story of Reignland: perhaps the first major
    move from Feris's religious comprehensive doctrine in a rela-
    tively homogeneous society is to a moral comprehensive doc-
    trine in a still relatively homogeneous Reignland under Juris,
    with a second move possible to less homogeneity with diverse
    comprehensive doctrines present.

4   Unsurprisingly, the view is somewhat more complicated. The subject of the overlapping consensus is the set of reasons acceptable for public discourse – hence, *public reasons*. Public reasons are then used to determine the principles of justice. For the sake of brevity, I will ignore this complication throughout.

5   It can be *reasonable* to reject a conclusion that it is not *rational* to reject when, for example, one holds false beliefs. Given a mistaken belief – perhaps one accepted for good reasons having to do with that belief's pedigree –it may be reasonable to reject a view one would otherwise accept.

6   Rawls suggests that the overlapping consensus would converge around the principles of justice he defends in 1971. If that is right, what is tolerated in a society that endorses his later (strictly political) view is the same as what is tolerated in a society that endorses his earlier (comprehensive doctrine) view. This is somewhat implausible, as the overlapping consensus in any given society would depend entirely on the comprehensive doctrines present in that society; with differing comprehensive doctrines, there would likely be different principles in the overlapping consensus. Rawls may think this unproblematic because he limits his theory to societies already liberal. I ignore this possibility in what follows, partly because I do not want to limit myself in that way.

7   See Book I of Locke's *An Essay Concerning Human Understanding*.

8   Note that if we emphasize the "as free and equal" clause, it would not matter what each individual would in fact endorse, but only what they would endorse *were they free and equal*. This, though, leaves Rawls essentially working with a hypothetical contract model like the one he used in 1971 and which is thus similarly reliant on a conception of the self that makes such a model possible – that is, we each must be capable of being as if free and equal.

9   Of course, it is. See Larmore 1999: 610; Hartley and Watson 2009: 497.

10   For more, see Gutmann 1985.

Chapter 3   The Harm Principle

1   The argument of this paragraph is meant to mirror a famous argument by David Lyons. He argues that rule utilitarianism devolves into act utilitarianism as the former can only endorse a rule that standardly creates the most utility for use in cases

where it does so; where an exception to that rule would create more utility, utilitarians must allow the exception. This is not genuine endorsement of a rule. See Lyons 1965: ch. 4.

2 Mill himself might not endorse the strict version of his principle. It's worth looking at Book V of his *Principles of Political Economy* to see some reasons for why this is so.

3 To clarify: I do not doubt that some propositions are subjective. For example, I believe "blue is a better color than orange," but I also take it to be a subjective statement. In such cases, though, I think there is no fact of the matter regarding the content of the belief, though there is a fact of the matter regarding my belief. That is, there is no objective truth about which is the better color – and so no truth about it at all. It is, though, objectively true that I take blue to be better than orange.

4 For a very different sort of example, consider false accusations. No one seriously thinks that an innocent person should be sentenced to jail time or death or any other penalty. Punishment is never for the innocent. We all take this to be objectively true, even if in some cases we do not know who is innocent. Consider an instance where you were accused of doing something bad that you did not do – surely, that no one else knew you were innocent had no impact on the truth of the matter.

5 Mill also calls indirect harms "constructive injuries," and Sidgwick calls them "secondary injuries." Both are problematic if we think of in*jur*ies as matters of *jur*isprudence, as we do here. (I also see no advantage in using "secondary" rather than "indirect.") I have been tempted to say indirect harms are "accepted hurts" – hurts one experiences only if one is willing to do so. (Harriett, at the end of this section, does not have to be hurt, but seems to choose to accept a role that leaves her pained.) This will not do, since we could say of almost anyone that they accept hurts; it's conceivable, after all, that an individual doesn't have to have their interests set back when a thief steals their money or when someone hits them with a bat – if only they would refuse to recognize that their interests were set back.

Chapter 4 Other Principles

1 Feinberg makes this explicit at the start of his book *Offense to Others* (1988: 2) as well as later in the book (1988: 94, etc.). Simester and von Hirsch think he does not pay enough attention to this (2002: 274).

2   In the case where everyone consents, the public health issue has no pull. Those on the bus during the event consent to being there, knowing what will happen, so if they get sick, they may get hurt, but by *Volenti,* they do not get harmed. Moreover, as the bus company agreed to allow the event to take place, they would be in a position to clean the bus completely after the event so that any public health issue would be their responsibility.

3   The benefit to others principle is reasonably considered part of liberalism. Importantly, different versions of liberalism can endorse different versions of the benefit to others principle. Locke, for an historical example, endorses both a principle of charity and an anti-waste proviso that limit just accumulations of property. See Cohen 2010.

4   Nonetheless, there is interference with a large group (taxpayers) that are not opposed. The advocate of the benefit to others principle thus must defend the view that interference with one to help another or to intervene with poverty is warranted. The harm principle, of course, would not warrant such interference unless – as will be discussed shortly – the poverty of the one benefited is caused by the taxpayers (or some reasonable subset thereof), since only then would they be doing the harm that warrants interference.

5   This is a broader understanding of the principle than Feinberg's. On his account, the principle indicates that it is "always a morally relevant reason in support of a proposed prohibition that it is necessary for the production of some *benefit* for persons other than the person who is prohibited" (1990: xx). Feinberg intends the principle to be only about criminal prohibitions. By contrast, here it is about any interferences – whether prohibitions or not and whether about legal crimes or not.

6   Some may think, "Wait, there is no interference here, only aid." I think this is mistaken for two reasons. First, aid is a form of interference. Second, and more to the point here, I am not talking of toleration of those in poverty, but toleration of the poverty itself (or, as we will see in a moment, of the system that causes or allows poverty).

7   In my view, toleration can be used to think about both welfare rights and taxation. Governments might oppose leaving people with all their income or assets because (some of) it can be better used collectively. The question I am encouraging in this section is: "What justifies that interference – that lack of toleration?" Those adopting the benefit to others principle think aiding the

poor does so. Those adopting the strict version of the harm principle believe that only harms do. The latter will recognize some taxation as legitimate – that needed to pay for things that are necessary for the prevention of harm, including military, police, and the like (as well as taxation needed to correct for past harms). Perhaps also that needed to compensate individuals somehow harmed by the collective, as I discuss next.

8   There might also be laws that are designed to encourage people to improve themselves or set forward their own interests. Such laws might be considered paternalist in a broad sense. We might also call them perfectionist: they seek to help people self-perfect. This is the point that paternalism and legal moralism (see next subsection) overlap, since in order to know if someone is self-perfecting, we need a notion of what their perfection is and this would presumably be a moral notion. (Ancient philosophy was often perfectionist in this sense: some idea of the perfect human person was defended and morality required pursuing that perfection.) We might keep paternalism and moralism separate at this point by insisting that there are two types of perfectionism: the paternalist version would only be about aiding a person in their pursuit of their own interests – whatever those pursuits happen to be – and the moralist version would be about pursuing an independently defended version of a perfected self. Notice also that either of these might be considered a variation of a benefit to others principle. Perhaps the paternalist version is a subjective benefit to others principle and the moralist version is an objective benefit to others principle. Clearly there are different ways to divide the territory here.

9   The accident resulting in his burns occurred in 1973; a documentary (*Dax's Case*) was made in 1984. See http://filmakers.com/index.php?a=filmDetail&filmID=157.

10 Consider also the case of Susan Potempa in 1993. Potempa lived in excruciating pain and sought and found – after at least four attempts – someone to kill her (see McConnell 2000: 8-9; Cohen 2007: 491ff).

11 See, for two examples, Dworkin 1972 and Rainbolt 1989.

12 It's worth noting a distinction between pure and impure paternalism. Impure paternalistic laws interfere with the activity of one agent in order to prevent *another* agent from hurting herself – e.g., a law disallowing the sale of narcotics is likely justified on paternalist grounds, but interferes with the seller (who is not hurting himself) rather than the buyer (who may be). By contrast, pure paternalist laws disallow the buying or

using of narcotics – that is, they disallow actions by those that would themselves be hurt. The difference is important, determining who must be interfered with to enforce the law.

13 See Sunstein and Thaler 2003 and 2008.

14 Some argue that Devlin only thought something somewhat less problematic: that changing the law to allow something that many believe is immoral would tear at the social fabric.

15 Stephen's view may be closer to Devlin's than I suggest here. He was concerned to defend liberty and thought restrictions on immoralities were necessary for this. Moreover, like Devlin, Stephen is concerned about the moral code that happens to be present in society (what we call "positive morality"), rather than objective morality. Like Devlin, too, he worries that without a protected moral code accepted within a society, that society would deteriorate.

16 I gather there are also religious claims that the marriage is immoral, but a (religious or other) claim is not an argument. Similarly, an argument that began with a premise that "God said X" would not be sufficient absent defense of the premises that (a) God exists and (b) that God said X. (Even that would not be sufficient, given the Euthyphro dilemma.)

17 The rest of this paragraph is adapted from Cohen 2004b: 413–16.

18 This is not, of course, always the case. There are times when a third party may know better than we do what our projects are. Indeed, there may be times when a third party confronts us with beliefs on these matters and we realize they are right. If, however, a third party insists that our project is X and we are convinced it is not, we have prima facie reason to disavow the third party's claim.

19 In my view, for example, one can act immorally without harming another by wrongly setting back one's own objective interests.

20 For one early (12/3/2003) report, see: news.bbc.co.uk/2/hi/3286721.stm.

21 See Judith Thurman's "Walking Through Walls: Marina Abramovic's Performance Art" in *The New Yorker*, March 8, 2010.

Chapter 5   Extending the Harm Principle

1 I say "tend to doubt" because I am not certain. It is clear that the environment has instrumental value: without it we would die. But does it have value other than that? One reason to think

it does is what is called the "last man argument," originally formulated by Richard Routley/Sylvan and subsequently explained by David Schmidtz (see Schmidtz and Willott 2002: xiii). The idea is simple: assume you are the last living human being on the planet and know it, and that you come across the last redwood tree on the planet (and you know it is the last). Most of us, Sylvan suggests, would recognize that it is wrong to chop down that majestic tree – though it serves no purpose for anyone. It thus seems to have non-instrumental value.

2   Many of us, though, would be prepared to tolerate the activity if it was part of a genuine experiment that promised important results that would further medical knowledge. Notice that nowhere am I talking about rights. I am not a rights theorist, but I am especially skeptical of the claim that nonhuman animals have rights. As will be indicated shortly, that does not mean it is OK to harm them.

3   Perhaps these are ideal interests; see chapter 6B.

4   Of course, there are people and processes that can be interfered with here. For example, we could require that homes be built to meet certain safety requirements, and that homeowners buy insurance for such situations, thereby interfering in a way meant to avoid setbacks to interest caused by things like tornadoes. This is all well and good, but one wonders what we would do if someone rationally wanted to live in a home – a tree house, perhaps – that could not meet such safety standards. I tend to think we must tolerate such behaviors. Paternalists, of course, would not. Importantly, of course, nothing I say here is meant as an argument against charity. While I would not give to a charity that aims to help those who build expensive homes on a faultline in California, I would likely give to a charity that aims to help poor victims of a hurricane.

5   This is not, of course, the whole story. Infanticide kills an infant and an infant is unlikely to have interests other than in not suffering. Still, there could be interests of others that are relevant. Presumably, women in general in that society have an interest in not being perceived as second-class citizens and perhaps the fact that the infanticide is always of female children encourages that perception. Additionally, it is plausible to talk of ideal interests of children – interests they have but do not know they have. Examples include adequate nutrition, love, shelter, etc. More on this in chapter 6B.

6   Given the high costs of military intervention, political leaders across the globe have unsurprisingly sought other ways to pressure foreign leaders. Economic embargos and international

sanctions are perhaps the most obvious examples. These are clearly attempts to interfere and so are not acts of toleration. Are they permissible acts of non-toleration? In the view defended here, of course, this depends on whether they are responses to harms or impending harms and what costs they impose.

7   Pogge calls this the "international resource privilege" of foreign leaders (2008: 118–22).

8   Pogge calls this the "international borrowing privilege" of foreign leaders (2008: 118–22).

9   See Pogge 2008: 159–72. See also http://www.healthimpactfund.org, and other work by Pogge.

10   Nor, though, is it unheard of. See Sulzbach 1940.

11   The age one ceases to be a minor (becomes a rational adult) – and so can consent – likely varies depending on what the issue is, since some issues require greater intellectual abilities and knowledge.

12   Interestingly, medicinal antibiotic use may need to be legally interfered with if the harm principle is accepted as the sole normative principle of toleration. Improper use of such drugs causes a public health risk – in the rise of so-called "super-bacteria" (antibiotic resistant bacteria) – that can cause harms to many. Though prescription drug laws (which are legal inter-ferences, and hence failures to fully tolerate, even though they are not fully prohibitive) are unlikely to completely eliminate the harms, they can help significantly.

13   For those that think this environmentally unfriendly, see Desrochers and Shimizu 2012.

14   This type of argument dates at least to Frédéric Bastiat's pamphlet "What is Seen and What is Not Seen," originally published in 1850.

15   Of course, there may not be friendlier environments available. This may make this situation exploitative. If such exploitation is harmful, interference would be permitted. If not, not. See Zwolinski 2007 and 2012. Clearly, these cases are similar to the international case of EPZs discussed in the previous subsection. The differences are clear, though: there, the treatment of employees is less voluntary and that treatment is further from the eyes of consumers.

16   This claim from large retailers may have the effect of keeping prices higher, since the incentive for smaller firms to compete on price is lowered.

17   Perhaps it would be acceptable for a salesperson to refuse to answer questions – that is, perhaps the restriction is only

against dishonest answers (and not non-answers). One wonders, though, why anyone would purchase an expensive item from a salesperson who refuses (or is unable) to answer relevant questions.

Chapter 6 Children and the Paradoxes of Toleration and Liberalism

1 We've basically considered two justifications for allowing parents to act as proxy for their children: consent of the child and the idea that the parents act in their child's interests. Another possibility is the idea that parents must be able to consent for their child in order to care for her. This account is problematic also. While the parent must be able to consent for their child in *some* matters, there is little reason to think this is true of *all* matters and the parent's claim is only likely to be challenged when it seems his or her action is not one of properly caring for the child, when the particular matter involved is one where the parent should not be able to consent for the child.

2 It's not (or not solely) a matter of luck for the parents. Good parenting takes time and effort. Parenting classes are readily available; every prospective parent should seek them out.

3 According to the National Center on Family Homelessness, "[m]ore than one in 45, or 1.6 million, children experience homelessness annually" (http://www.homelesschildrenamerica .org/media/203.pdf). According to the US State Department, "[e]ach year, an estimated 600,000–800,000 men, women, and children are trafficked across international borders." Half of these are children (see pages 6 and 15 at http://www.state.gov/ documents/organization/34158.pdf). That is, 300,000–400,000 children are *sold* across borders (this does not include those sold within a single country).

4 It may be that the best approach here is to look at the capabilities approach defended by Amartya Sen and Martha Nussbaum. See, e.g., Sen 1995.

5 We might say that endorsement of the harm principle (or any principle of toleration) is a failure to remain utterly neutral, but this purported move away from some chimerical neutrality is not a significant move. If we must consider this an endorsement of a conception of the good, we must recognize it is endorsement of an extremely thin conception of the good that allows people to live as they like – so long, only, as they do not harm others. (Put differently, this still seems like a form

of neutralism more than a form of what philosophers call perfectionism.)

6   The first part of this paragraph is adapted from Cohen 2013: 5159.

Chapter 7   General Defenses of Toleration

1   See Forst 2008 (esp. at p. 105) for more on this line of argument from Bayle. See also Kilcullen 1988: esp. chs 2 and 4.

2   This should be read, I think, as including a normative principle of toleration similar to Mill's harm principle. In Locke's *Second Treatise of Government* (ch. II, §6), we are told: "being all equal and independent, no one ought to harm another."

3   For an interpretation of Locke making his view seem even closer to Bayle's, see Tuckness 2008.

4   Recall that a harm is a *wrongful* setting back of interests. While saving X's soul may be *helping* X, failure to save X's soul (when under no special obligation to do so) is not *harming* X.

5   For a related argument, see Sher 1995: esp. 150.

6   So standard advice to job-seekers: *pretend* you are confident about your ability to do a job you are interviewing for and, if necessary, continue pretending as you do the job. You may end up doing the job successfully – and confidently.

7   I do not mean here to be endorsing reliabilism or any specific epistemological view.

8   I believe I owe the argument of this paragraph to Gene Mills and I thank him for it.

9   See Goldman 1999 (particularly at p. 189) for an argument that such gatekeepers can improve the overall level of truth acquisition. See Fallis 2000 and 2004 for responses to Goldman that mirror what I say here.

10   This example is not entirely fictitious. The Creation Evidence Museum in Glen Rose, Texas (led by Carl Baugh, who claims man coexisted with dinosaurs) is but one example. See www.creationism.org for a list.

11   See Rachels 1999: ch. 2, and Knorpp 1998 for more on relativism.

12   The roots of this argument can also be found in Mill 1978[1859]: 16–20.

13   This is not far from my own view, as I hope is clear. I am convinced we should tolerate when the harm principle says we must, but I admit I am fallible and may be wrong. However, I will hold to the belief – recognizing it may be a mistake – until given good reason not to.

14 It is not a stance open to the subjectivist, for there is no reason for him to think he is ever mistaken – he is always right so long as he proposes what he genuinely believes, since his genuine belief in P makes P true (for him). The cultural relativist, on the other hand, can be wrong – but only by misunderstanding what is genuinely believed in his culture.

15 For more on this, see Rawls 1971: §78 and Lomasky 1987: ch. 3. See also Schmidtz 1995 on "maiuetic" ends.

16 See Kukathas's discussion of Australian Aborigines (2003: 102). My example is meant to be similar to his real-world case, but only similar.

17 The argument of this section is developed from my 2004b where it receives only one paragraph.

18 Some might worry that this argument and that from autonomy in section A above rehearse the arguments for autonomy presented in chapter 4D. There is, though, a clear connection between toleration and freedom in general (which allows for the ability to act on one's conscience, to act autonomously, and to provide innovations to society). Early liberals defended toleration after all, to defend liberty.

19 If one means by "pluralism" that *anything* could be of value and thus takes the view that everything must be tolerated, one would need arguments as to how things that seem obviously to have only disvalue (e.g., rape) are nonetheless values to be tolerated. No serious thinker defends such a view.

20 To see the point of the parenthetical, consider that the plausible moral value of religious commitment does not carry the requirement that diverse religious views are endorsed or tolerated (nor does it mean opposing such diversity). The moral value can be had with or without diversity.

21 This argument follows straightforwardly from Ricardian economics, with its emphasis on comparative advantage. See Muldoon et al. 2012.

Chapter 8 Conclusion

1 The next two paragraphs are adapted from Cohen 2007: 497–8.

2 Many have commented that we do not want to be merely tolerated but want to be embraced, or at least fully respected. I do not deny this, but note that we are never dissatisfied with being tolerated if we are not; it is only when we are at least tolerated that we think we want more (and some may never want more).

References

Archard, David William. 2003. *Children, Family and the State*. Burlington, VT: Ashgate Publishing.

Barry, Brian. 2001. *Culture and Equality*. Cambridge, MA: Harvard University Press.

Bayle, Pierre. 2005[1688]. *A Philosophical Commentary on These Words of the Gospel, Luke 14:23, "Compel Them to Come In, That My House May Be Full."* Indianapolis, IN: Liberty Fund.

Berry-Dee, Christopher and Steven Morris. 2010. *Online Killers*. Berkeley, CA: Ulysses Press.

Bok, Derek. 2010. *The Politics of Happiness*. Princeton: Princeton University Press.

Brock, Gillian. 2009. *Global Justice: A Cosmopolitan Account*. Oxford: Oxford University Press.

Ciepley, David. 2013. "Beyond Public and Private: Toward a Political Theory of the Corporation." *American Political Science Review* 107: 139–158.

Cohen, Andrew Jason. 2004a. "What Toleration Is." *Ethics* 115: 68–95.

Cohen, Andrew Jason. 2004b. "Defending Liberalism Against the Anomie Challenge." *Social Theory and Practice* 30: 391–427.

Cohen, Andrew Jason. 2007. "What the Liberal State Should Tolerate Within Its Borders." *Canadian Journal of Philosophy* 37: 479–513.

Cohen, Andrew Jason. 2010. "A Conceptual and (Preliminary) Normative Exploration of Waste." *Social Philosophy and Policy* 27(2): 233–273.

Cohen, Andrew Jason. 2013. "Toleration." In Hugh LaFollette, ed., *International Encyclopedia of Ethics*. Oxford: Blackwell Publishing, pp. 5150–5160.

Cohen, Joshua. 2009. "Truth and Public Reason." *Philosophy & Public Affairs* 37(1): 2–42.

Cowen, Tyler. 2002. *Creative Destruction*. Princeton: Princeton University Press.

Creppell, Ingrid. 2002. *Toleration and Identity: Foundations in Early Modern Thought*. New York: Routledge.

Desrochers, Pierre and Hiroko Shimizu. 2012. *The Locavore's Dilemma*. New York: PublicAffairs Books.

Devlin, Patrick. 1968. *The Enforcement of Morals*. Oxford: Oxford University Press.

Dick, Caroline. 2011. *The Perils of Identity: Group Rights and the Politics of Intragroup Difference*. Vancouver: UBC Press.

Dworkin, Gerald. 1972. "Paternalism." *The Monist* 56: 64–84.

Eisenberg, Avigail. 1994. "The Politics of Individual and Group Difference in Canadian Jurisprudence." *Canadian Journal of Political Science* 27(1): 3–21.

Fallis, Don. 2000. "Veritistic Social Epistemology and Information Science." *Social Epistemology* 14: 305–316.

Fallis, Don. 2004. "Epistemic Value Theory and Information Ethics." *Minds and Machines* 14: 101–117.

Feinberg, Joel. 1984. *Harm to Others*. New York: Oxford University Press.

Feinberg, Joel. 1986. *Harm to Self*. New York: Oxford University Press.

Feinberg, Joel. 1988. *Offense to Others*. New York: Oxford University Press.

Feinberg, Joel. 1990. *Harmless Wrongdoing*. New York: Oxford University Press.

Forst, Rainer. 2008. "Pierre Bayle's Reflexive Theory of Toleration." In Melissa Williams and Jeremy Waldron, eds., *Nomos XLVIII: Toleration and Its Limits*. New York: New York University Press, pp. 78–113.

Galeotti, Anna Elisabetta. 2002. *Toleration as Recognition*. Cambridge: Cambridge University Press.

Goldman, Alvin I. 1999. *Knowledge In a Social World*. Oxford: Clarendon Press.

Gutmann, Amy. 1985. "Civic Education and Social Diversity," *Ethics* 105(3): 557–579.

Hampton, Jean. 1989. "Should Political Philosophy Be Done without Metaphysics?" *Ethics* 99: 791–814.

Hansmann, Henry and Reinier H. Kraakman. 1991. "The Uneasy Case for Limiting Shareholder Liability in Tort." *Yale Law Journal* 100: 1879–1934.

Hansmann, Henry, Reinier Kraakman, and Richard Squire. 2006. "Law and the Rise of the Firm." *Harvard Law Review* 119(5): 1333–1403.

Hart, H. L. A. 1963. *Law, Liberty and Morality*. Stanford: Stanford University Press.

Hartley, Christie and Lori Watson. 2009. "Feminism, Religion, and Shared Reasons: A Defense of Exclusive Public Reason." *Law and Philosophy* 28: 493–536.

Kilcullen, John. 1988. *Sincerity and Truth: Essays on Arnauld, Bayle, and Toleration*. Oxford: Clarendon Press.

Knorpp, William Max Jr. 1998. "What Relativism Isn't." *Philosophy* 73(284): 277–300.

Kukathas, Chandran. 2003. *The Liberal Archipelago*. New York: Oxford University Press.

Larmore, Charles. 1999. "The Moral Basis of Political Liberalism." *Journal of Philosophy* 96(12): 599–625.

Locke, John. 1993[1865]. "A Letter concerning Toleration" In David Wooten, ed., *Political Writings of John Locke*. New York: Penguin Books, pp. 390–436.

Lomasky, Loren. 1987. *Persons, Rights, and The Moral Community*. New York: Oxford University Press.

Lyons, David. 1965. *Forms and Limits of Utilitarianism*. Oxford: Oxford University Press.

McConnell, T. 2000. *Inalienable Rights: The Limits of Consent in Medicine and the Law*. New York: Oxford University Press.

MacIntyre, Alasdair. 1984. *After Virtue*, 2nd ed. Notre Dame, IN: University of Notre Dame Press.

Marx, Karl. 2001[1875]. *Critique of the Gotha Program*. Rockville, MD: Wildside Press.

Mill, J. S. 1978[1859]. *On Liberty*. Indianapolis, IN: Hackett Publishing.

Mills, Claudia. 1998. "Choice and Circumstance." *Ethics* 109: 154–165.

Muldoon, Ryan, Michael Borgida, and Michael Cuffaro. 2012. "The Conditions of Tolerance." *Politics, Philosophy, & Economics* 11: 322–344.

Nadler, Steven. 1999. *Spinoza: A Life*. Cambridge: Cambridge University Press.

Newey, Glen. 1999. *Virtue, Reason and Toleration: The Place of Toleration in Ethical and Political Philosophy*. Edinburgh: Edinburgh University Press.

Pateman, Carol. 1988. *The Sexual Contract*. Cambridge: Polity.

Pogge, Thomas. 2008. *World Poverty and Human Rights*, 2nd ed. Cambridge: Polity.

Rachels, James. 1999. *The Elements of Moral Philosophy*. New York: McGraw-Hill.

Rainbolt, George W. 1989. "Prescription Drug Laws: Justified Hard Paternalism." *Bioethics* 3(1): 45–58.

Rawls, John. 1971. *Theory of Justice*. Cambridge, MA: Harvard University Press.

Rawls, John. 1977. "The Basic Structure as Subject." *American Philosophical Quarterly* 14(2): 159–165.

Rawls, John. 1993. *Political Liberalism*. New York: Columbia University Press.

Rawls, John. 1999. "The Idea of Public Reason Revisited." In Samuel Freeman, ed., *Collected Papers*. Cambridge: Harvard University Press, pp. 573–615.

Raz, Joseph. 1986. *The Morality of Freedom*. Oxford: Oxford University Press.

Sandel, Michael. 1982. *Liberalism and the Limits of Justice*. Cambridge: Cambridge University Press.

Scanlon, T. M. 1996. "The Difficulty of Tolerance." In David Heyd, ed., *Toleration: An Elusive Virtue*. Princeton: Princeton University Press, pp. 226–239.

Schmidtz, David. 1995. *Rational Choice and Moral Agency*. Princeton: Princeton University Press.

Schmidtz, David and Robert Goodin. 1998. *Social Welfare and Individual Responsibility*. Cambridge: Cambridge University Press.

Schmidtz, David and Elizabeth Willott. 2002. *Environmental Ethics: What Really Matters, What Really Works*. New York: Oxford University Press.

Sen, Amartya. 1995. "Capability and Well-Being." In Martha Nussbaum and Amartya Sen, eds., *The Quality of Life*. Oxford: Clarendon Press, pp. 30–53.

Sher, George. 1995. "Liberal Neutrality and The Value of Autonomy." *Social Philosophy and Policy* 12: 136–159.

Simester, A. P. and Andrew von Hirsch. 2002. "Rethinking the Offense Principle." *Legal Theory* Volume 8(3): 269–295.

Sulzbach, Walter. 1940. "Tolerance and the Economic System." *Ethics* 50(3): 290–313.

Sunstein, Cass R. and Richard H. Thaler. 2003. "Libertarian Paternalism Is Not an Oxymoron." *University of Chicago Law Review* 70(4): 1159–1202.

Sunstein, Cass R. and Richard H. Thaler. 2008. *Nudge: Improving Decisions about Health, Wealth, and Happiness*. New Haven, CT: Yale University Press.

Taylor, Charles. 1989. *Sources of the Self*. Cambridge: Cambridge University Press.

Tuckness, Alex. 2008. "Locke's Main Argument for Toleration." In Melissa Williams and Jeremy Waldron, eds., *Nomos XLVIII: Toleration and Its Limits*. New York: New York University Press, pp. 114–138.

Waldron, Jeremy. 1988. "Locke: Toleration and the Rationality of Persecution." In Susan Mendus, ed., *Justifying Toleration: Conceptual and Historical Perspectives*. Cambridge: Cambridge University Press, pp. 61–86.

Wall, Steven. 2003. "The Structure of Perfectionist Toleration." In Steven Wall and George Klosko, eds., *Perfectionism and Neutrality: Essays in Liberal Theory*. Lanham, MD: Rowman and Littlefield, pp. 231–255.

Weinstock, Daniel M. 1994. "The Political Theory of Strong Evaluation." In James Tully, ed., *Philosophy in the Age of Pluralism: The philosophy of Charles Taylor in question*. Cambridge: Cambridge University Press, pp. 171–193.

Young, Iris Marion. 1990. *Justice and the Politics of Difference*. Princeton: Princeton University Press.

Zwolinski, Matt. 2007. "Sweatshops, Choice, and Exploitation." *Business Ethics Quarterly* 17: 689–727.

Zwolinski, Matt. 2012. "Structural Exploitation." *Social Philosophy and Policy* 29: 449–472.

Index